ORDINARY PEOPLE
WITH AN
EXTRAORDINARY WITNESS

The Word
—IN—
LIFE™
BIBLE
DISCOVERY
Series

Exploring ACTS

THOMAS NELSON PUBLISHERS
Nashville • Atlanta • London • Vancouver

ORDINARY PEOPLE WITH AN EXTRAORDINARY WITNESS
Word In Life™ Bible Discovery Guide
to Exploring Acts

© 1996 by Thomas Nelson Publishers

Published in Nashville, Tennessee, by Thomas Nelson, Inc.

Written by Joseph Snider.

Printed in the United States of America
1 2 3 4 5 6 7 8 — 00 99 98 97 96

CONTENTS

INTRODUCTION
The Word In Life:
God's Word, Your Life

Someone has well said that Scripture was not written merely to be studied, but to change our lives. James exhorts us to be 'doers of the word, and not hearers only' (James 1:22), and Jesus said, 'By this My Father is glorified, that you bear much fruit; so you will be My disciples' (John 15:8). Clearly, the point of God's Word is not to make us 'smarter sinners' but to help us become more like Jesus Christ by making the Word of God part of our lives.

However, applying biblical truth in this day and age is far from easy. In the first place, the fact that the Bible was written thousands of years ago in a different culture can sometimes make it difficult to understand. And even if we grasp what the writers were saying to their original readers, we still must make the connection to our own situation today. In the end, many people wonder: Can Scripture really make any difference in our complex, modern world? Yes it can, and this publication helps to show the way.[1]

If the soil of your heart is prepared for planting, studying God's Word is like seeding a whole garden. The seed is good, so expect a bountiful harvest!

But if the soil of your heart is resistant, the Word can be like a hammer breaking down barriers to the truth. Don't be surprised if the Word knocks you about some.

Fire is another metaphor for God's Word. It purifies, exposing and removing dross in order to reveal the value of what was there all along.

The Word of God also puts songs on your lips—songs of praise to God for His goodness, or songs of contentment that all is well between you and God.

The Word In Life Bible Discovery Guide *is designed to help you plant the seeds, to give you wisdom for understanding the constructive hammer blows and purifying flames, to show you the score for the song—to help you hear and understand God's Word in your life. This Guide will help you to*

- Observe life in the Word—in the stories and sayings, people, places, and events of the Bible.
- Explore their meaning for then and now, for there and here.
- Personalize their meaning for you, today; and
- Experience the Word in your life!

Keyed to the innovative, user-friendly Word In Life Study Bible, *this Guide will help you use its features to the max (although you can also use it with any Bible). And the Guide is designed for individual use and for use by small groups (with a section for leaders).*

Like the Word In Life Study Bible *itself, this* Bible Discovery Guide *is concerned with understanding and applying the Bible to daily life. Look for emphasis upon applying God's Word to your work and your public life as well as to your character and your personal relationship with Jesus Christ.*

Enjoy the Word of God. Let it get into your life and make it deep and rich in the wisdom and character of God as revealed in His Son and applied by His Holy Spirit.

1. *The Word In Life™ Study Bible: New Testament Edition* (Nashville, TN: Thomas Nelson Publishers, 1993), vii.

"POWER TO THE PEOPLE!"

Acts 1:1-11

Power! Power to the people! Power to the people! Right on!" chanted swarms of students on countless college campuses during the late 1960s. That slogan meant many things at different levels. To some people it meant nothing. The demonstration was a "happenin' thing" where they had fun. To others, it was a personal cry. They wanted some control over a war that was taking friends to a ghostly world of napalm and death. To John Lennon it was a song lyric.

Supposedly, "Power to the people!" was a challenge to oppressive institutions to leave ordinary people alone so they could choose their own futures without coercion. It assumed that government was too big. That industry was money-hungry. That "little people" were regularly victimized by the powerful. That minority groups were exploited by the unfeeling majority. Watch classic period movies, such as *Easy Rider,* and you get the mood of the time.

The book of Acts opens with a promise of "Power to the people!" that has none of the undertones of resentment or confrontation that marked the counterculture of the 60's. Acts opens with a straightforward promise by Jesus of power—power that would propel messengers to witness about Jesus Christ to the very ends of the earth. Those who heard Him had no idea how much hope and joy were hidden in that promise. The 60's never delivered on their promise of "Power to the people!" Jesus did.

◆ ◆ ◆ ◆ ◆ ◆ ◆ ◆

—— ◆ BLOCKBUSTER SEQUEL ◆ ——
(Acts 1:1–3)

The maximum length of a first-century parchment scroll was 32 to 35 feet.[1] The book of Acts pretty much filled a scroll of maximum length. Acts is the sequel to an earlier book, the longest of the New Testament, that must have crammed its scroll completely full. What did the author say was the purpose of the "prequel" to Acts? (Acts 1:1, 2)

. . . .

. . . .

. . . .

Compare Acts 1:1–3 with Luke 1:1–4. What features of these introductory passages suggest that the book of Acts is the sequel to the Gospel of Luke?

. . . .

. . . .

◆ ◆ ◆ ◆ ◆ ◆ ◆ ◆

CONSIDER THIS

Read the *Word in Life Study Bible (WILSB)* feature "Luke, The Gentile Author" (Introduction to Luke). "A Greek from Antioch of Syria (according to one tradition), he was well educated and thoroughly acquainted with the Roman world. His writings, the Gospel of Luke and Acts, show a far more cultured form of Greek than the rest of the New Testament." What credentials for writing his books do the following passages suggest?

◆ Luke 1:1–3

. . . .

. . . .

◆ Acts 16:10–17; 20:5–21:18; 27:1–28:16 (the "we" passages)

. . . .

. . . .

◆ Colossians 4:14; 2 Timothy 4:11; Philemon 24

. . . .

. . . .

Theophilus was a common name of first-century Jews living in cities with strong Greek cultures. It meant "Loved by God." The title "most excellent" (Luke 1:3) had a formal meaning when applied to nobility (see Acts 23:26; 24:3; 26:25). Either Theophilus was a very prominent person or Luke was being very courteous to him. The dedication to a prominent person of books meant to be read widely has been a common practice down to the modern era.

In Acts 1:2, 3, what did Luke indicate were the final subjects of his "former account"?

. . . .

. . . .

What features of Luke 24:36–53 align with the look back in Acts 1:2, 3?

. . . .

. . . .

Luke wrote that the resurrected Jesus talked with His disciples about the kingdom of God (Acts 1:3). In Luke there are about 40 explicit references to the kingdom of God. Look up the following passages and record what you learn about the kingdom of God.

◆ Luke 1:33

. . . .

. . . .

◆ Luke 11:2

. . . .

. . . .

◆ Luke 12:31

. . . .

. . . .

◆ Luke 17:20, 21

. . . .

. . . .

◆ Luke 18:16, 17

. . . .

. . . .

◆ Luke 19:11–27

. . . .
. . . .

◆ Luke 21:29–33

. . . .
. . . .

◆ ◆ ◆ ◆ ◆ ◆ ◆ ◆

Circle the letter of the statement that best captures your response to the teaching of Jesus in Luke about the kingdom of God.

a. It's a mystery to me.

b. The kingdom is the here-and-now spiritual reign of Christ in human hearts.

c. The kingdom of God is a future literal kingdom when Jesus returns.

d. All of the above.

e. None of the above. I think the kingdom of God is

. . . .

◆ ◆ ◆ ◆ ◆ ◆ ◆ ◆

——— ◆　　Blockbuster Story　　◆ ———

"Tradition has assigned this book the title, 'The Acts of the Apostles' as if Peter, Paul, and a handful of other spiritual giants alone carried out the significant work of the early church. But the account shows that the Holy Spirit *and a lot of ordinary people* took the message of Christ 'to the end of the earth.'

"This is one of the most timely books, because it illustrates what happens when everyday people, filled with God's power, apply their faith to everyday life and society."[2]

Before Jesus ascended to heaven He outlined for His disciples the broad stages of the spread of the gospel by everyday people under the empowerment of the Holy Spirit. Read Acts 1:8 and list the three predicted phases of gospel expansion.

1. . . . .

2. . . . .

3. . . . .

◆ ◆ ◆ ◆ ◆ ◆ ◆ ◆

CONSIDER THIS

Read the *WILSB* feature "Opportunities Look Like Barriers" (Acts 1:4). What obstacles did the early church face in taking the gospel to each of the areas listed in Acts 1:8?

◆ Phase One

. . . .

. . . .

◆ Phase Two

. . . .

. . . .

◆ Phase Three

. . . .

. . . .

Although Acts is the story of "the Holy Spirit and a whole lot of ordinary people" taking the gospel to the end of the earth, Luke highlighted the activity of an apostle associated with Jewish believers and another apostle associated with Gentile believers. Who was the apostle associated with Jewish believers? (see Acts 1:15–22; 2:14–41; 3:1—4:23; 5:3–10; 8:14–25; 9:32—11:18; 12:3–17; 15:6–11, 14)

. . . .

. . . .

Who was the apostle associated with Gentile believers? (see Acts 9:1–30; 11:25–30; 12:25—28:31)

. . . .

. . . .

In between the two major characters of Acts are found two transitional characters. Look up the following passages and identify them.

◆ Transitional character one (Acts 6:1—7:60)

. . . .

. . . .

◆ Transitional character two (Acts 8:1–40)

. . . .

. . . .

Based on the passages you already looked up, how do the two main characters and two transitional characters in the book of Acts relate to the three phases of gospel expansion outlined in Acts 1:8 and carried out through the rest of the book?

◆ Phase One

. . . .

. . . .

◆ Phase Two

. . . .

. . . .

◆ Phase Three

. . . .

. . . .

◆ ◆ ◆ ◆ ◆ ◆ ◆ ◆

🔍 A CLOSER LOOK

Current biblical scholarship pays a great deal of attention to Luke—Acts. The best theory is that "originally the two volumes circulated together as two parts of one complete writing. But during the late first or early second century, the first volume became associated with the Gospels identified with Matthew, Mark, and John, thus forming the fourfold Gospel. Luke's second volume was left to go its own way. It was at this time, it seems, that the second volume received its present title."[3]

Read the *WILSB* feature "The Second of Two Volumes" (Introduction to Acts). "The book ends abruptly, leading some scholars to suggest that Luke was working on or at least had planned a third installment." What two purposes does this feature suggest Luke may have hoped to accomplish with Acts?

1. . . . .

. . . .

2. . . . .

. . . .

THE WORLD OF THE EARLY CHURCH

CONSIDER THIS

Read the *WILSB* feature "Christ Collides with Culture" (Introduction to Acts). "Acts shows the gospel's impact on a variety of cultures and societies as it builds into a movement. It internationalizes across gender, ethnic, lingual, geographic, occupational, and economic boundaries."

Locate the places mentioned in the feature "Christ Collides with Culture" on the map. Mark each prominently with a highlighter or colored marker.

Why do you think the Holy Spirit directed the gospel of Jesus Christ in the first years of the church to these dangerous, bustling centers of diverse cultures rather than to safer, quieter settings?

. . . .

. . . .

——— ◆ BLOCKBUSTER SUSPENSE ◆ ———
(Acts 1:4–11)

When you already know the end of a story it's hard to realize how much uncertainty about the future the characters experienced while caught in the flow of events. Forty days after Jesus was resurrected from the dead, His apostles were understandably eager to know what was going to happen as a result of this spectacular turn of events. They were especially anxious to know how "the kingdom of God" (Acts 1:3) would express itself.

The apostles had not stayed in Jerusalem during the entire 40 days of Jesus' post-resurrection appearances. They had returned to their homes in Galilee (Matt. 28:7, 16–20; John 21). Toward the end of the 40 days, the disciples returned to Jerusalem and assembled once more in the upper room where so many unusual things had occurred (Acts 1:4).

What was the main point of Jesus' final instruction to the apostles in the upper room? (Acts 1:4–5; see Luke 24:49).

. . . .

. . . .

In the Old Testament, predictions about the outpouring of the Holy Spirit usually concerned the restoration of the Davidic kingdom in Israel (see Is. 32:15; 44:3; Ezek. 36:25–28; 39:29; Joel 2:28—3:1). Jesus had spoken after the Last Supper in quite literal terms of a kingdom for Israel with thrones and state banquets (Luke 22:29–30). What seems to have been in the apostles' minds as they asked Jesus about the kingdom? (Acts 1:6)

. . . .

. . . .

What seems to have been in Jesus' mind as He answered the apostles' question about the kingdom? (Acts 1:7–8).

. . . .

. . . .

Why did Jesus not want the apostles speculating about timing of the future kingdom of God? (Acts 1:7; see Mark 13:32–33).

. . . .

. . . .

What dangers exist for us if we try to create detailed scenarios about the end times from biblical prophecies?

. . . .

. . . .

Instead of the timing of the future kingdom, what two things did Jesus want His apostles to be concerned about in the near future? (Acts 1:8).

1. Getting . . . .

. . . .

2. Giving . . . .

. . . .

◆ ◆ ◆ ◆ ◆ ◆ ◆ ◆

CONSIDER THIS

Read the *WILSB* feature "Power" (Acts 1:8). "At the beginning of Acts, Jesus' followers appear confused and fearful. But by the end of the book they are well on their way to transforming the Roman world with the gospel. What accounts for this dramatic change?"

In what ways is the power from the Spirit not the kind of power the world might want to have?

. . . .

. . . .

In terms of all that Jesus had told them just before the ascension, why do you think it was important for the apostles to know that He would physically return some day? (Acts 1:11)

. . . .

. . . .

As you contemplate the meaning of your life and work, what difference does it make that Jesus will come again?

. . . .

. . . .

1. Craig S. Keener, *The IVP Bible Background Commentary: New Testament* (Downers Grove, IL: InterVarsity Press, 1993), 323.

2. "Introduction to Acts," *The Word in Life Study Bible* (Nashville, TN: Thomas Nelson Publishers, 1993), 401.

3. Richard N. Longenecker, "The Acts of the Apostles," *The Expositor's Bible Commentary,* Vol. 9 (Grand Rapids, MI: Zondervan Publishing House, 1981), 207.

THE WITNESS GROWS AT HOME
Acts 1:12—5:42

At first the worldwide witness to Jesus empowered by the Holy Spirit was no more than a variation of Judaism. Neither the apostles nor the Jewish leaders nor the everyday residents of Jerusalem knew what to make of the rapidly growing movement they called "the Way" (Acts 9:2).

The followers of Jesus wanted to convince all of their fellow countrymen to accept Him as their Messiah and personal Savior. For their part the Jewish faithful expected the followers of "the Way" quietly to blend in with the many and varied subgroups of Judaism.

There was bound to be trouble when the followers of "the Way" proved to be exclusivists about Jesus. "There is no other name under heaven given among men by which we must be saved," they insisted (Acts 4:12).

THE WORLD AT YOUR DOORSTEP

Acts 1:12—2:47

Richard Halliburton was an explorer and adventurer born in the year 1900. He climbed a tower of the Golden Gate Bridge while it was under construction. He swam the length of the Panama Canal. He flew an open-cockpit biplane with the king of Jordan. He visited every exotic place on earth that he could. He died in 1939 during a typhoon in the China Sea while trying to cross the Pacific Ocean in a handbuilt Chinese junk.

"When I was a boy in school my favorite subject was geography, and my prize possession my geography book," Halliburton wrote in the preface to one of his adventure books. "This book was filled with pictures of the world's most wonderful cities and mountains and temples, and had big maps to show where they were. I loved that book because it carried me away to all the strange and romantic lands. I read about the Egyptian Pyramids, and India's marble towers, about the great cathedrals of France, and the ruins of ancient Babylon. The stories of such things always set me to dreaming, to yearning for the actual sight and touch of these world wonders."[1]

Before Richard Halliburton felt the urge to go to the ends of the world, the ends of the world came to him in the form of a book. Before the apostles of Jesus Christ took their witness about the Lord to the ends of the world, the Lord brought the ends of the world to them during the celebration of the Jewish feast of Pentecost.

◆ ◆ ◆ ◆ ◆ ◆ ◆ ◆

───── ◆ INGREDIENT ONE: WITNESSES ◆ ─────
(Acts 1:12–26)

In the first two chapters of Acts, God created in Jerusalem a miniature version of the new society of believers in Jesus Christ that He planned to call out of every nation, people, and language of the earth. The recipe for this new society contained three ingredients, the first of which was a group of witnesses to the life and ministry of Jesus.

The Mount of Olives, or Olivet (Acts 1:12), was a ridge running north and south along the east side of Jerusalem. The scribes applied the law to permit travel of about a kilometer on the Sabbath. When the apostles returned this short distance to Jerusalem after Jesus ascended to heaven, what did they do? (Acts 1:12–14)

. . . .

. . . .

Calculate the amount of time the disciples waited for the coming of the Holy Spirit. It was 50 days from Passover to Pentecost. Subtract the time Jesus was in the tomb and the number of days between His resurrection and ascension (Acts 1:3).

. . . .

. . . .

◆　◆　◆　◆　◆　◆　◆　◆

♡ CONSIDER THIS

Read the *Word in Life Study Bible (WILSB)* feature "An Inclusive Prayer Meeting" (Acts 1:14). "The first prayer group was notable for its inclusiveness, particularly of women."

Why do you think the apostles immediately welcomed women into their deliberations and prayers when other Jewish groups did not?

. . . .

. . . .

Peter applied passages from two psalms (Pss. 69:25; 109:8) to Judas Iscariot. The psalms are about evil men and false friends. Judas epitomized both of those groups. What conclusions did Peter reach from these psalms? (Acts 1:15–17, 20)

. . . .

. . . .

◆　◆　◆　◆　◆　◆　◆　◆

☑ FOR YOUR INFO

Read the *WILSB* feature "Field of Blood" (Acts 1:19), Acts 1:18, 19, and Matthew 27:3–10. "The tragic end of Judas Iscariot, who betrayed Jesus (see Matt. 26:14), was memorialized in the purchase of a plot of ground for a cemetery, appropriately named the Field of Blood" (Acts 1:19).

How can you reconcile Matthew's account that Judas hanged himself and Luke's report that his body burst open from a fall?

. . . .

. . . .

How can you reconcile Matthew's statement that the priests bought the field (Matt. 27:7) with Luke's claim that Judas bought it (Acts 1:8)?

. . . .

. . . .

Jesus had chosen twelve apostles to represent Himself and the kingdom of God to their fellow Jews. Twelve was a number representative of the totality of Israel, which had begun with twelve tribes originating from the sons of Jacob.

What were the qualifications to be one of the twelve apostles? (Acts 1:21, 22)

. . . .

. . . .

Who decided which disciples should be considered to replace Judas? (Acts 1:23)

. . . .

. . . .

How did the apostles allow the Lord to choose who should replace Judas? (Acts 1:24–26)

. . . .

. . . .

What did the apostles need to be able to bear witness about? (Acts 1:21, 22)

. . . .

. . . .

What do you need to be able to bear witness of?

. . . .

. . . .

Circle the letter of the statement that you think best applies the lessons of Acts 1:21–26 to choosing church leaders today.

a. You need two equally qualified candidates for every office so it ultimately doesn't matter which one is selected.

b. Never replace a qualified leader unless he commits a really serious sin.

c. Leaders should be nominated on the basis of biblical qualifications and selected prayerfully by a culturally appropriate method.

d. Leaders should be chosen by some sort of blind draw that only God can influence.

e. Existing leaders should act as God's spokespersons for selecting all new leaders.

◆ ◆ ◆ ◆ ◆ ◆ ◆ ◆

◆ INGREDIENT TWO: THE SPIRIT ◆
Acts 2:1–13

The second ingredient in the Lord's recipe for creating a new society was the empowerment of the witnesses by the Holy Spirit. John the Baptist, years before, had predicted the crucial role the Spirit would play in the total ministry of Jesus (Luke 3:16). Jesus had pointed to the Spirit as the Comforter and Counselor for His followers (John 14:16, 17, 26; 16:7–15). Finally, Jesus had urged the apostles to wait in Jerusalem after His ascension for the coming of the Spirit (Luke 24:49; Acts 1:4, 5, 8).

Describe the events of the Day of Pentecost according to the actions of the following (Acts 2:1–8):

◆ The disciples

. . . .

. . . .

◆ The Holy Spirit

. . . .

. . . .

◆ The onlookers

. . . .

. . . .

◆ ◆ ◆ ◆ ◆ ◆ ◆ ◆

CONSIDER THIS

Read the *WILSB* feature "A Surprising First Fulfillment" (Acts 1:8). The harvest feast of Pentecost brought together thousands of Jews (including converts to Judaism) from all over the Roman Empire. This made it possible to bring about at least a partial fulfillment of the promise of Acts 1:8—that the gospel would spread 'to the end of the earth'—much sooner than the apostles expected."

What parts of the world were represented by the Jewish pilgrims at the feast of Pentecost? (Acts 2:9–11)

. . . .

. . . .

What did Luke specify about the pilgrims from Rome, the capital of the empire? (Acts 2:10)

. . . .

. . . .

◆ ◆ ◆ ◆ ◆ ◆ ◆ ◆

CONSIDER THIS

Read the *WILSB* feature "Pluralism at Pentecost" (Acts 2:5). "An international, multilingual church was born when the onlookers heard the gospel preached and believed it."

What are the barriers in modern culture that churches have to overcome to build congregations of different ethnic and racial backgrounds?

. . . .

. . . .

What do you think the Holy Spirit would have to do in your church to break through these barriers?

. . . .

. . . .

◆ ◆ ◆ ◆ ◆ ◆ ◆ ◆

——— ◆ INGREDIENT THREE: ◆ ———
THE MESSAGE
Acts 2:14–39

The third ingredient in the Lord's recipe for creating a new society was a message about the Person and work of the resurrected Jesus. Once the witnesses were empowered by the Holy Spirit they boldly proclaimed the Lord and salvation through His name. Peter's sermon on Pentecost represents the earliest example of ideas and Scripture used to draw unbelievers to faith in Jesus.

Before Peter spoke about Jesus, he explained the wondrous occurrence that had attracted the crowd and stirred its curiosity. How did Peter explain what had happened? (Acts 2:14–21)

. . . .

. . . .

What facts of Jesus' life did Peter mention briefly for the crowd who would have been familiar with Him? (Acts 2:22–25)

. . . .

. . . .

How did Peter reason from Psalm 16:8–11 and Psalm 110:1 that David wrote about Jesus rather than himself? (Acts 2:25–35)

. . . .

. . . .

What did Peter's conclusion to his sermon contain about each of these topics? (Acts 2:37)

◆ Truth about Jesus

. . . .

. . . .

◆ Personal responsibility

. . . .

. . . .

◆ ◆ ◆ ◆ ◆ ◆ ◆ ◆

CONSIDER THIS

Read the *WILSB* feature "Carrots, Not Sticks" (Acts 2:37–38). "Notice that Peter did not call for an immediate response. Only after God's Spirit had `cut to the heart' those in the audience and they asked for help (v. 37) did he explain what they ought to do."

Why do you think the listeners in Jerusalem responded to what Peter said about Jesus with such urgency?

. . . .

. . . .

How can you be sensitive to times when the Holy Spirit wants you to urge someone to respond and times when He wants you to witness without pressing for a commitment?

. . . .

. . . .

◆ ◆ ◆ ◆ ◆ ◆ ◆ ◆

—— ◆ RESULT: A NEW SOCIETY ◆ ——
Acts 2:40–47

The final verses of Acts 2 provide one of the few New Testament descriptions of a congregation of believers in Jesus Christ. It is an exciting, appealing, and challenging portrait that makes you want to plunge further into Acts to see what God accomplished through this group of people. Clearly the Holy Spirit established a committed society that served its Lord with enthusiasm and joy.

Keeping in mind that "perverse" means "distorted" or "crooked," why do you think Peter called the population of Jerusalem at that time "a perverse generation"? (Acts 2:40)

. . . .

. . . .

In what ways are people today "a perverse generation"?

. . . .

. . . .

◆ ◆ ◆ ◆ ◆ ◆ ◆ ◆ ◆

☑ FOR YOUR INFO

Read the *WILSB* feature "Off to a Good Start" (Acts 2:1). "Pentecost took its name from the fact that it occurred . . . fifty days after Passover. Each family offered thanks to God for the just-completed grain harvest by giving the firstfruits of its produce to the temple priests. . . . On this day, . . . 3,000 people responded to Peter's proclamation of the gospel (Acts 3:41), becoming the firstfruits of the church."

Why do you think these 3,000 new believers in Jesus from all over the eastern Mediterranean world remained together in Jerusalem for a while instead of returning immediately to their homes?

. . . .

. . . .

What benefits do you gain from frequent contacts with groups of Christians that you can't get from private study and worship?

. . . .

. . . .

◆ ◆ ◆ ◆ ◆ ◆ ◆ ◆

♀ CONSIDER THIS

Read the *WILSB* feature "New Life Means New Lifestyles" (Acts 2:42–47). "The converts from Peter's sermon remained in Jerusalem for a while, perhaps as guests of the handful of local believers. They celebrated their new life in Christ in five important ways (vv. 42–47)." How do you celebrate your life in Christ in each of the following ways found in Acts 2:42–47?

◆ Studying the apostles' doctrine

. . . .
. . . .

◆ Sharing fellowship meals

. . . .
. . . .

◆ Worshiping God with praise

. . . .
. . . .

◆ Sharing possessions with each other

. . . .
. . . .

◆ Caring for each other's needs

. . . .
. . . .

What impact did the transformed life of the first believers in Jesus have on the people around them? (Acts 2:47)

. . . .
. . . .

What qualities do you think Christians in your community need to demonstrate to make a forceful impact on the general public?

. . . .
. . . .

◆ ◆ ◆ ◆ ◆ ◆ ◆ ◆

CONSIDER THIS

Read the *WILSB* feature "Reconnecting Sunday and Monday" (Acts 2:46–47). "Does the faith you celebrate on Sunday sometimes feel disconnected from the 'real world' you face on Monday? The newly formed group of believers (vv. 46–47) closed that gap by practicing a rhythm of two kinds of experiences—

gathering for growth and worship balanced by scattering into the world for work and to communicate the gospel to non-Christian friends and coworkers."

Believers Gathered for Refinement	Believers Scattered for Engagement
Donate money from asset sales to care for their poor (4:36–37).	
Discipline those who practice deceit in giving to the poor (5:1–11).	
	Meet in public to care for the sick; many are converted (5:12–21).
	Are arrested and tried on charges of civil disobedience (5:22–42).
	Go to the Samaritans with the gospel; challenge Simon, a leading sorcerer (8:3–13).
Meet to discuss and confirm Samaritan work (8:14–17).	
Discipline a new believer for misuse of Holy Spirit (8:18–24).	
	Take the gospel to an Ethiopian government official on a highway (8:26–40).
Confirm and nurture the new faith of Saul (9:10–22).	
Accept Saul into the fellowship, even though he had persecuted them (9:26–28).	

What opportunities does your church offer you to gather for growth and worship?

. . . .
. . . .

As you examine the practices of the infant society of believers in Jesus at the end of Acts 2, which of these practices do you need to strengthen in your life to become a more balanced Christian?

. . . .
. . . .

1. Richard Halliburton, *Richard Halliburton's Complete Book of Marvels* (Indianapolis, IN: The Bobbs-Merrill Company, 1941), 1.

GROWING PAINS

Acts 3:1—5:42

Poor Alice in Wonderland had the worst imaginable growing pains. She didn't know whether she would shrink to the size of a mouse or expand until she was too large to fit in the room. Her erratic growth occurred because she did not know what would happen when she drank from the bottle labeled "DRINK ME" or ate from the cake labeled "EAT ME." She experimented with each, trying to reach the right size to get the golden key from the glass table and follow the White Rabbit through the little door, but nothing ever worked predictably in Wonderland.

The fledgling church in the early chapters of Acts was in Jerusalem rather than Wonderland, but nothing happened very predictably there either. Many people respected the followers of Jesus and listened eagerly when they talked about Him. But a growing number of influential people resented the growth and popularity of the Way. Why wasn't everyone in Jerusalem enthusiastic about the risen Lord?

Even inside the group of believers some strange things began to happen. Some people felt neglected. Others wanted honor and recognition. The solution to these problems wasn't easy. Why couldn't everyone in the Way remain united in their initial enthusiasm for the risen Lord?

♦ ♦ ♦ ♦ ♦ ♦ ♦ ♦

♦ SHARING THE POWER OF ♦
JESUS' NAME
(Acts 3:1–26)

No one in Jerusalem questioned the commitment of the followers of Jesus to the Jewish laws and customs. Their attitudes and practices relative to first-century Judaism did not distinguish them from the people around them. But they were distinguished by what they said about Jesus and what they did in His name. Skim through Acts 3—5 and highlight or circle every occurrence of the term "name" when it refers to Jesus. How many did you find? _____

What characteristics or qualities of Jesus seem to be summed up in these uses of the word "name"?

. . . .

. . . .

◆ ◆ ◆ ◆ ◆ ◆ ◆ ◆ ◆

CONSIDER THIS

Read the *Word in Life Study Bible (WILSB)* feature "Jesus—The Name You Can Trust" (Acts 3:1). "Using none of the sophisticated marketing strategies of today's corporate giants, a small-town carpenter's name managed to become a byword in the first-century world."

What kind of power did the name of Jesus prove itself to have in Acts 3—5?

. . . .

. . . .

How could you express more confidence in the name of Jesus in your personal life, in the workplace, and in your witness for Him?

. . . .

. . . .

Peter and John were engaged in their daily routine—praying in the temple at 3:00 P.M., the time of the evening sacrifice. The lame man was engaged in *his* daily routine—begging at the Beautiful Gate between the court of the Gentiles and the court of the women on the east side of the temple complex. Describe the healing of the lame man (Acts 3:3–8, 16).

. . . .

. . . .

Describe the reactions of the following people to the healing in the name of Jesus.

◆ The lame man (Acts 3:8, 11)

. . . .

. . . .

◆ The multitude (Acts 3:9–11)

. . . .

. . . .

◆ The Sadducean authorities who did not believe in resurrection from the dead (Acts 4:1–7, 15-22)

. . . .
. . . .

◆ ◆ ◆ ◆ ◆ ◆ ◆ ◆

CONSIDER THIS

Read the *WILSB* feature "Seizing the Opportunity" (Acts 3:12). "People today may be just as surprised by social or personal changes that God brings about. . . . We can help `open the eyes' of others to see God's hand behind what they have observed, the way Peter did."

How did Peter keep the attention on the Lord and away from himself when he seized the opportunity to talk about Jesus? (Acts 3:12–16)

. . . .
. . . .

How can you keep the attention on the Lord rather than yourself when you explain how God has been at work in your life?

. . . .
. . . .

What situations do you think make good opportunities to be seized for talking about the presence and work of the Lord?

. . . .
. . . .

List all of the names or designations Peter gave Jesus in Acts 3:12–26.

. . . .
. . . .

What do these names tell you about Jesus?

. . . .
. . . .

Evidently, Peter still anticipated the momentary return of Jesus to establish the kingdom with His throne in Jerusalem. How did this expectation affect the appeal Peter made to his listeners in Solomon's Porch? (Acts 3:19– 21, 25–26)

. . . .
. . . .

◆ ◆ ◆ ◆ ◆ ◆ ◆ ◆

──── ◆ DEFENDING THE NAME OF JESUS ◆ ────
(Acts 4:1–31)

The same Sadducean authorities who had spearheaded the execution of Jesus turned their attention to His followers when Peter and John healed the lame man and created a notable commotion in the temple. The powerful priests were used to intimidating people with shows of their authority. They were greatly surprised at the response of these Galilean fishermen who had been with Jesus.

The Sanhedrin usually sat in a semicircle so the council could focus clearly on those who addressed it. Peter and John were put in the "hot seat" and grilled. Why do you think the Sadducees asked about the power and the name Peter and John acted in when they healed the lame man? (Acts 4:7)

. . . .

. . . .

How did Peter's reply answer the question of the Sanhedrin? (Acts 4:8–12)

. . . .

. . . .

How did Peter's response put him in charge and the Sanhedrin on the defensive?

. . . .

. . . .

◆ ◆ ◆ ◆ ◆ ◆ ◆ ◆

CONSIDER THIS
Read the *WILSB* feature "MYTH: It Doesn't Matter What You Believe, All Religions Are Basically the Same" (Acts 4:12). "Peter describes the exclusiveness of Christianity by claiming that there is no other name that can save (v. 12). That doesn't play well in our pluralistic society where tolerance is a chief virtue."

Why do so many people want to believe that all religions will get you to God?

. . . .

. . . .

Why is Christianity an exclusive faith system?

. . . .

. . . .

If you were trying to witness to a friend who believed that it doesn't matter what a person believes, where would you begin in order to present the Christian point of view?

· ·

· ·

What factors did the Sanhedrin take into account when it reached its decision? (Acts 4:13–17)

· ·

· ·

What was its ruling? (Acts 4:17–18)

· ·

· ·

How did Peter and John respond to the Sanhedrin's ruling? (Acts 4:19–20)

· ·

· ·

When they heard of it, how did the rest of the followers of Jesus respond to the Sanhedrin's treatment of Peter and John? (Acts 4:23–28)

· ·

· ·

How did the community of believers in Jesus pray in the face of opposition from the powerful people who had killed Jesus? (Acts 4:29–30)

· ·

· ·

How do you think Christians today should balance proper respect for human and divine authority without becoming either cowardly or arrogant?

· ·

· ·

◆ ◆ ◆ ◆ ◆ ◆ ◆ ◆

CONSIDER THIS

Read the *WILSB* feature "Being Renewed and Renewed" (Acts 4:31). "Like the Christians in Acts, we need to gather regularly for spiritual refueling."

What groups do you count on as sources of spiritual strength and encouragement?

. . . .

. . . .

The Lord answered the prayer of the disciples visibly (Acts 4:31). If your church prayed earnestly for courage and boldness, what do you think the answer of the Lord would look like?

. . . .

. . . .

◆ ◆ ◆ ◆ ◆ ◆ ◆ ◆

—— ◆   FEARING THE NAME OF JESUS   ◆ ——
(Acts 4:32—5:16)

The followers of the Way experienced a surge of growth after the healing of the lame man in the temple. That growth was marked by reverence and awe for the power of the name of Jesus. The Lord made it clear to everyone that following Him was not only the way to forgiveness and great blessing but also a path of great responsibility and integrity.

◆ ◆ ◆ ◆ ◆ ◆ ◆ ◆

CONSIDER THIS
Read the *WILSB* feature "Sharing Things in Common" (Acts 4:32–35). "Reading about these early Christians, modern believers are challenged to consider: Do we, with our much higher standard of living, show the same commitment to generosity as these believers?"

How did the early believers regard their possessions and people in need?

. . . .

. . . .

What did the power of the name of Jesus have to do with their generosity?

. . . .

. . . .

What do you think are the major hindrances to powerfully expressive generosity within your church?

. . . .

. . . .

Who is the most generous Christian you know? How is that person's witness for Christ affected by that generosity?

. . . .

. . . .

◆ ◆ ◆ ◆ ◆ ◆ ◆ ◆ ◆

💡 CONSIDER THIS

Read the *WILSB* features "Wealth—Hold It Lightly" (Acts 4:37—5:11) and "Ananias and Sapphira—Playing Games with God" (Acts 5:1–11). "God calls us as believers to hold our resources lightly. . . . He gives [them] to us as a trust to be managed—not a treasure to be hoarded."

Contrast the ways in which Barnabas, on the one hand, and Ananias and Sapphira, on the other, handled their resources when other believers in Christ were in need.

◆ Barnabas (Acts 4:36–37)

. . . .

. . . .

◆ Ananias and Sapphira (Acts 5:1–2, 8)

. . . .

. . . .

◆ How might Christians today deceitfully try to appear more generous than they are?

. . . .

. . . .

What are some ways that generosity can be an encourager within your church or other Christian community? Can you give examples of generous people who are an encouragement to others?

. . . .

. . . .

God judged Ananias and Sapphira very severely for their deceitfulness during the infancy of the community of believers in Christ (Acts 5:1–10). He did the same to Achan, who introduced deception into Israel at the very beginning of the conquest of Canaan (Josh. 7). Why do you think God demonstrated so forcefully in both cases the necessity of integrity for the success of a people calling themselves by His name?

. . . .
. . . .

◆ ◆ ◆ ◆ ◆ ◆ ◆ ◆

♀ CONSIDER THIS

Read the *WILSB* feature "A Confusing Reputation" (Acts 5:12–16). "Seeing loyalty to God's kingdom often triggers peculiar responses from unbelievers. Many will keep a safe distance, . . . while others enthusiastically join up."

When the apostles did many signs and wonders in Jerusalem, what was the enthusiastic response of the masses? (Acts 5:12–16)

. . . .
. . . .

What cautious reaction lay below the surface of popular enthusiasm? (Acts 5:11, 13)

. . . .
. . . .

How do you think we should treat unbelievers who are interested in Christ but are very cautious about committing to Him?

. . . .
. . . .

◆ ◆ ◆ ◆ ◆ ◆ ◆ ◆

──── ◆ SUFFERING FOR THE ◆ ────
NAME OF JESUS
(Acts 5:17–42)

Jewish law required that ordinary citizens be warned clearly in the presence of witnesses concerning any offense and its consequences before they could be punished.[1] Once the Sanhedrin had admonished Peter and John, they felt legally free to carry out their threats of action against the Way. Their only concern was the high regard in which the populace held the followers of Jesus. They had found a way to execute Jesus; they would find a way to make His disciples suffer.

Because the apostles continued to preach and perform miracles in the name of Jesus (Acts 5:12–16) in disobedience of the Sanhedrin's command to desist from those practices (4:18–21), the Sadducean leader became angry and had all the apostles imprisoned (5:17–18).

When the Lord sent an angel to free the apostles, why do you think He sent them to the temple to teach rather than into hiding? (Acts 5:20, 25)

. . . .

. . . .

How do you think the council felt when they found the prison secure but empty and the prisoners teaching about Jesus in the temple? (Acts 5:22–26)

. . . .

. . . .

How would you summarize each of the following?

◆ The charge of the Sanhedrin (Acts 5:28)

. . . .

. . . .

◆ Peter's response (Acts 5:29–32)

. . . .

. . . .

◆ ◆ ◆ ◆ ◆ ◆ ◆ ◆

CONSIDER THIS

Read the *WILSB* feature "We Ought to Obey God Rather Than Men" (Acts 5:22–32). "What should Christians do when faced with a conflict between human authority and God's authority?"

When Christians feel required by God's Word to disobey human authority in order to obey God, what should their attitude be toward each of these?

◆ The goal of their actions

. . . .

. . . .

◆ The human authorities they will disobey

. . . .

. . . .

◆ The consequences of their actions

. . . .

. . . .

Why do you think the attitude of the Sadducees toward the apostles had become murderous? (Acts 4:21; 5:17, 33)

. . . .

. . . .

Gamaliel was a famous first-century Pharisee. Pharisees often opposed the Sadducean majority on the Sanhedrin. They accepted the doctrine of resurrection from the dead and opposed all compromises with the Romans. How did Gamaliel advise the council to approach the uncooperative followers of Jesus? (Acts 5:34-39)

. . . .

. . . .

What did the Sanhedrin hope to achieve by having the apostles flogged? (Acts 5:40)

. . . .

. . . .

What was the result of the flogging the council gave the apostles? (Acts 5:41–42)

. . . .

. . . .

What is the worst indignity you have ever suffered for being a follower of Jesus?

. . . .

. . . .

If you knew you were going to face physical persecution because of your faith, what changes do you think you would need to make in your thoughts and behavior to prepare for it?

. . . .

. . . .

1. Richard N. Longenecker, "Acts," *The Expositor's Bible Commentary*, Vol. 9 (Grand Rapids, MI: Zondervan Publishing House, 1981), 300.

THE WITNESS REACHES
THE NEIGHBORS

Acts 6:1—11:18

The middle chapters of Acts often confuse readers. They contain interesting stories, but the pattern and purpose of those stories taken together isn't always so clear. The initial growth of the infant church in Jerusalem in Chapters 2 through 5 and the missionary activity of Paul into the Gentile world from Chapter 13 on are straightforward enough. What, however, are Stephen, Philip, and Peter up to in between?

The turmoil of Acts 6—11 is the tumultuous labor pains leading up to the birth of a Christian church that can exist anywhere and include anyone. These stories tell how God taught the apostles and other disciples to witness to people very different from themselves.

4

KICKED OUT OF THE HOUSE

Acts 6:1—8:3

Francesco Bernadone grew up in the highlands of Italy's Apennine Mountains near beautiful Lake Trasimeno and the Tiber River valley. His father was a wealthy Italian businessman, and his mother was a beautiful young French girl. As Francesco grew up, he lavished his father's money on playboy friends and charmed every pretty girl around with the love songs of two romantic nations.

His father despaired at his son's wastefulness, but he determined to make a businessman of him. Francesco was charming and persuasive—surely he would tire of being a playboy. Perhaps time in the army would discipline his mind and heart.

And it did. Francesco came home from military action with a totally unexpected interest in God. When he began to give away his possessions, that was too much for his father. He had been willing to wait while Francesco wasted his money on fast living, but he would not keep quiet while his son gave it away to help the poor.

Peter Bernadone forcibly locked his son in a closet in the hopes he would give up his crazy religious notions. When Francesco escaped, his father told him never to come home again. Within a year Francis of Assisi and a band of twelve like-minded followers quietly began to transform the corrupt morals of the thirteenth-century Italian church by the example of their simple lives.

In first-century Jerusalem, the leaders of Jewish temple ritual were willing to put up with many things from the followers of Jesus. They could claim that Jesus was the Messiah. They could operate as a distinct sect within the larger fold of Judaism. But they could not attack the traditions that had grown up around Moses and the temple. That would get them "thrown out of the house."

◆ ◆ ◆ ◆ ◆ ◆ ◆

—— ◆ A SERVANT WITH A SERMON ◆ ——
(Acts 6:1–15)

In Jerusalem lived many Jews who had been born elsewhere before immigrating. These "Hellenistic" Jews had grown up less strictly and were looked down on by the homegrown "Hebrew" Jews. Apparently many Hellenistic Jews responded to the gospel of Jesus because it promised them first-class status. They were disappointed to find the same biases operating within the community of believers in Jesus.

◆　◆　◆　◆　◆　◆　◆　◆

CONSIDER THIS

Read the *Word in Life Study Bible (WILSB)* feature "Society's Divisions Affect Believers" (Acts 6:1). "How are divisions in our culture revealed in our churches, at work, and in our neighborhoods? How does the gospel of Jesus challenge these attitudes?"

Why is it difficult if not impossible to avoid reflecting some of the sinful and divisive attitudes and practices of the culture we live in?

. . . .

. . . .

How can we become better at identifying attitudes and practices in our culture that are contrary to God's will?

. . . .

. . . .

What are some attitudes and practices common in churches around you that need evaluation in light of God's will?

. . . .

. . . .

◆　◆　◆　◆　◆　◆　◆　◆

A CLOSER LOOK

Widows were traditionally cared for with special funds established by the synagogue to which the extended family belonged. The followers of Jesus accepted responsibility for widows within their number. Read the *WILSB* feature "A Growing Movement Confronts Ethnic Tensions" (Acts 6:2–6). "Success never means the end of problems: it just means a new set of problems."

How did the apostles see that the problem of caring for widows impartially was solved rather than shoved aside?

. . . .

. . . .

Why was it important to involve Hellenist Jewish leaders in dealing with the problem?

. . . .

. . . .

What problems do you or your church face because of success? How can you manage these problems in a way that serves people and honors God?

. . . .

. . . .

What happened when the followers of Jesus involved seven Hellenist leaders to resolve an ethnic problem that no other group in Jerusalem had successfully dealt with? (Acts 6:7)

. . . .

. . . .

Because Stephen and his coworkers were selected on the basis of spiritual qualification (Acts 6:3), it isn't surprising that he also had a spiritual as well as a service ministry within the community of Hellenistic Jews (v. 8). A synagogue of Hellenistic Jews, former slaves from Africa and Asia Minor, became his chief opponents (v. 9). What did Stephen's opponents do when they couldn't debate him successfully? (Acts 6:11–15)

. . . .

. . . .

The charge brought against Stephen (Acts 6:13–14) was an exaggeration and distortion of things he had said. How have you heard people around you exaggerate or distort what you or other Christians say?

. . . .

. . . .

How can you respond at times like that so that people will be reminded of the angels? (Acts 6:15)

. . . .

. . . .

◆ ◆ ◆ ◆ ◆ ◆ ◆ ◆

WRONG ABOUT THE LAND
(Acts 7:1–29)

 "Before the Fall of Jerusalem in A.D. 70, the three great pillars of popular Jewish piety were (1) the land, (2) the law, and (3) the temple."[1] When Stephen spoke to the Sanhedrin, he did not defend himself against the charges made by the Synagogue of the Freedmen. When the high priest asked, "Are these things so?" Stephen systematically confronted his listeners about each of the three pillars of piety and challenged their attitudes toward Jesus.

First, Stephen told the Sanhedrin they placed too much emphasis on the promised land. What momentous events in the history of Israel did Stephen point out happened outside the promised land during the lives of these great men?

◆ Abraham (Acts 7:2–8)

. . . .

. . . .

◆ Joseph (Acts 7:9–16)

. . . .

. . . .

◆ Moses (Acts 7:17–29)

. . . .

. . . .

How do Christians today sometimes place too much emphasis on God's activity within their "land"—their country, their denomination, their church?

. . . .

. . . .

◆ ◆ ◆ ◆ ◆ ◆ ◆ ◆

WRONG ABOUT THE LAW
(Acts 7:30–43)

 Next, Stephen told the Sanhedrin that they made an idol of the law but failed to do what God commanded them to do. He emphasized Moses as the representative of the law—a representative whom Israel too easily and often rebelled against in the past and the present.

What authority had the Lord given Moses in establishing Israel as a nation under God's law? (Acts 7:30–38)

. . . .

. . . .

How did Stephen establish that ancient Israel had rejected Moses? (Acts 7:35, 38–43)

. . . .

. . . .

How did Stephen connect Jesus to Moses as an authority rejected by Israel? (Acts 7:37)

. . . .

. . . .

How can Christians today compromise the authority of the Word of God and reject His commands even while they think they are biblical?

. . . .

. . . .

Which commands or teachings of the Bible do you find hardest to accept? How can you improve your understanding of difficult Scriptures and how can you strengthen your commitment to accept and obey all God has said?

. . . .

. . . .

◆ ◆ ◆ ◆ ◆ ◆ ◆ ◆

_____ ◆ WRONG ABOUT THE TEMPLE ◆ _____
(Acts 7:44–53)

Finally, Stephen sealed his doom by questioning the importance of the temple in Jerusalem for the purposes of God. Other Jewish splinter groups criticized the established leaders for being wishy-washy spiritually and not obeying the law rigorously enough, but nobody in first-century Judaism questioned the centrality of the temple. Earlier, the Sanhedrin had tried to use Jesus' temple views against Him (Matt. 26:60–61). They were eager to do the same to Stephen (Acts 6:14).

What positive things did Stephen have to say about the portable tabernacle built at Mount Sinai? (Acts 7:44–46)

· ·

· ·

What implied criticisms did Stephen make of the permanent temple in Jerusalem? (Acts 7:47–50)

· ·

· ·

When have you seen Christians focus on a church building so much that their focus on the Lord suffered?

· ·

· ·

What do you think is the proper attitude for Christians to have toward church buildings and other places dedicated to the worship of God?

· ·

· ·

How many different charges did Stephen make against the Jewish leadership in the Sanhedrin? (Acts 7:51–53)

· ·

· ·

Compare Stephen's concluding blast against the Sanhedrin (Acts 7:51–53) to Peter's statement in Acts 5:29–32. What makes Stephen's so much harsher?

· ·

· ·

Under what circumstances can you imagine the Holy Spirit prompting you to rebuke someone as strongly as Stephen rebuked the Sanhedrin?

· ·

· ·

◆ ◆ ◆ ◆ ◆ ◆ ◆ ◆

◆ A SURGE OF PERSECUTION ◆
(Acts 7:54—8:3)

It was more socially acceptable for the Sanhedrin to condemn a Hellenistic Jew than a Hebraic one. Legally, the Sanhedrin needed Roman approval to execute Stephen, but in the passion of the moment they did it and got away with it. Suddenly, it became acceptable and popular to persecute believers in Jesus—especially the Hellenistic ones. Not surprisingly, a leader of the persecution emerged and flexed his newfound muscles.

How did the dignified leaders of Judaism behave in the council room at the end of the defense of Stephen? (Acts 7:54, 57)

. . . .

. . . .

How did the Lord prepare Stephen for the ordeal of martyrdom that faced him? (Acts 7:55–56)

. . . .

. . . .

Jesus had been crucified because Romans executed Him; Stephen was stoned because Jews executed him. The methods differed, but how were the reactions of Stephen to execution similar to Jesus' reactions to His death? (Acts 7:59–60, see Luke 23:32–49)

. . . .

. . . .

◆ ◆ ◆ ◆ ◆ ◆ ◆ ◆

CONSIDER THIS

Read the *WILSB* feature "Resistance—Unpopular Obedience" (Acts 7:57–60). "Before you engage in potentially costly causes, make sure you are sacrificing for the right thing."

What are the typical consequences of championing unpopular causes?

. . . .

. . . .

How can you keep a loving and serving attitude toward those who oppose you while you support an unpopular cause?

. . . .

. . . .

What intensification of the involvement of Saul in the persecution of believers in Jesus occurs through the three references to him in this section? (Acts 7:58; 8:1, 3)

· ·

· ·

◆ ◆ ◆ ◆ ◆ ◆ ◆ ◆ ◆

☑ FOR YOUR INFO

Read the _WILSB_ feature "Saul of Tarsus" (Acts 13:2–3). "Apparently the incident with Stephen galvanized [Saul's] commitment to traditional Judaism and set him off on a mission to seek out and destroy as many believers as he could."

What feature does each of the following Scriptures add to the portrait of Saul?

◆ Acts 21:39

· ·

· ·

◆ Acts 22:3

· ·

· ·

◆ Philippians 3:4–6

· ·

· ·

◆ Acts 8:3

· ·

· ·

What was the result of the persecution that broke out after the martyrdom of Stephen? (Acts 8:1)

· ·

· ·

◆ ◆ ◆ ◆ ◆ ◆ ◆ ◆ ◆

☿ CONSIDER THIS

Read the _WILSB_ feature "The Message Leaves Jerusalem" (Acts 8:1). "Jerusalem served chiefly as a launching pad for the gospel—quite a contrast from its role as the center of gravity for the worship of God in the Old Testament."

From Stephen's message to the Sanhedrin, what would you conclude about the Lord's ability to minister to people outside of Jerusalem and the land of Judea?

. . . .

. . . .

A few years ago, few people suspected that thousands of missionaries would be active in the former Soviet Union. Where in the world are some places that are very resistant to the gospel?

. . . .

. . . .

What are some ways the gospel can get into those places today?

. . . .

. . . .

What do you think would need to happen for those places to become receptive to the gospel of Jesus Christ?

. . . .

. . . .

What would God have to do to make you a missionary to that part of the world?

. . . .

. . . .

1. Richard N. Longenecker, "The Acts of the Apostles," *The Expositor's Bible Commentary*, Vol. 9 (Grand Rapids, MI: Zondervan Publishing House, 1981), 337.

THE GOSPEL MAKES STRANGE BEDFELLOWS

Acts 8:4—9:31

From the English Channel to the Swiss Alps, all was truly quiet on the Western Front in France on Christmas Eve of 1914. The war was only five months old, but already 800,000 men had been wounded or killed. Trenches reached within fifty miles of Paris. Every soldier wondered whether Christmas Day would bring another round of fighting and killing.

But on that Christmas Eve, before the "War to End All Wars" had brutalized its combatants and destroyed the innocent optimism of the twentieth century, peace broke out spontaneously. British soldiers raised Merry Christmas signs above the barbed wire and shell craters. Carols wafted back and forth in German, French, and English.

Christmas dawned and here and there soldiers left their trenches over the protests of officers and met in no-man's land. There, little knots of uniformed enemies chatted, sang, and exchanged impromptu gifts of sweets and cigars. Along miles of the front,

an eerie Christmas peace hung in the air. In one muddy field between the lines, British soldiers played soccer against German troops, who won, three to two.

The next day, the war sputtered back to life in most sectors, but here and there opposing units refused to open fire and lose the peace of Christmas. But as fresh forces arrived and commands rotated, the Christmas peace quickly faded away. The high commands of both armies issued orders that further "informal understandings" with the enemy be punished as treason.[1]

Whenever and wherever men and women come face to face with Jesus and His gospel, they find that He brings together enemies to make them friends. Peace reigns whenever and wherever we will let the gospel do its work, especially among enemies transformed by its power.

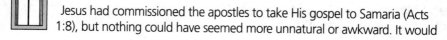

◆ THE NASTY NEIGHBORS ◆
(Acts 8:4–25)

Jesus had commissioned the apostles to take His gospel to Samaria (Acts 1:8), but nothing could have seemed more unnatural or awkward. It would be hard to make friends with your neighbors if you had spent years running their kids out of your yard, making fun of them to everyone else on the block, and dumping your trash over their fence. But God used a tragedy to break through deep-seated hostility between Jews and Samaritans long enough for the gospel of Jesus to do its work.

❖ ❖ ❖ ❖ ❖ ❖ ❖ ❖

💡 **CONSIDER THIS**

Read the *Word in Life Study Bible (WILSB)* feature "Jews Have No Dealings with Samaritans" (John 4:9). "There are countless modern parallels to the Jewish-Samaritan enmity—indeed, wherever peoples are divided by racial and ethnic barriers. Perhaps that's why the Gospels and Acts provide so many instances of Samaritans coming into contact with the message of Jesus."

How had hatred developed through the centuries between Jews and Samaritans? (see 2 Kings 17:29–1; Ezra 9:1–10:44)

. . . .·. . . . .

. . . .

Who are the people with whom you prefer to have no dealings? How can you confront your attitudes and begin to change them?

. . . .

. . . .

Stephen and Philip are the transitional characters in Acts between Peter the apostle to the Jews and Paul the apostle to the Gentiles. Stephen paid with his life to reveal that the Way was not just another sect of Judaism. Philip invested his life to show that the gospel was meant for people who weren't full-blooded Jews. Philip stayed close to Judaism—Samaritans and Gentile adherents to Jewish beliefs—but he opened the door for Paul's ministry to genuine pagans.

Describe the scenario of Philip's ministry in Samaria and the response of the Samaritans. (Acts 8:5–8)

. . . .

. . . .

❖ ❖ ❖ ❖ ❖ ❖ ❖ ❖

💡 **CONSIDER THIS**

Read the *WILSB* features "Simon—Infatuated with Power" (Acts 8:9–24) and "Give Me Power!" (Acts 8:18–19). "Simon illustrates a common habit of new believers—trying to use their newfound faith to justify old, sinful habits, or, in their zeal, 'help God out.'"

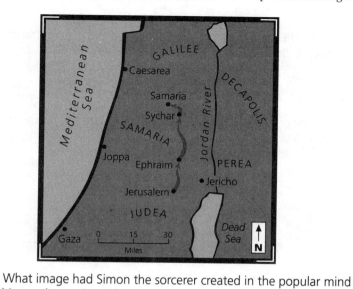

What image had Simon the sorcerer created in the popular mind through his occult practices? (Acts 8:9-11)

· ·

· ·

How did Simon's interest in personal power interfere with his ability to trust Jesus?

· ·

· ·

In what area(s) of life do you need to guard against the temptation to pursue power and prestige? Why?

· ·

· ·

CONSIDER THIS

Read the *WILSB* feature "The Conversion of Samaritans to the Gospel—and of Peter and John to Samaritans" (Acts 8:4–25). "News of the revival reached the apostles in Jerusalem, and they dispatched Peter and John to investigate. The two Galileans must have been stunned and no doubt humbled by what they found."

How did God establish the equality of the Samaritan believers with the Jewish believers?

· ·

· ·

How did the apostolic role in Samaria insure the unity of the infant church? (Acts 8:14–17)

. . . .

. . . .

What do you think Peter and John learned about the power of the gospel of Christ to overcome racial and ethnic barriers? What makes you think they learned these lessons?

. . . .

. . . .

◆ ◆ ◆ ◆ ◆ ◆ ◆ ◆

——— ◆ THE EAGER ENVOY ◆ ———
(Acts 8:26–40)

The Samaritans were bitter enemies of the Jews, but they at least had some Jewish blood in their veins. Gentiles, on the other hand, were total- ly unclean. Fervent Jews avoided all nonessential contact with Gentiles. In the first century there were many Gentiles who converted to Judaism or followed Jewish beliefs without going through the conversion ceremony. The latter was known as "God fearers." The first Gentile convert to faith in Jesus was either a Jewish convert or a God fearer. Philip once again was the evangelist.

The persecution following the death of Stephen had transported Philip to Samaria. How did the Lord guide Philip with regard to the Ethiopian eunuch? (Acts 8:26–27, 29)

. . . .

. . . .

YOU ARE THERE

Read the *WILSB* feature "Ethiopia" (Acts 8:27). Biblical Ethiopia was not the same territory and people as modern Ethiopia. Biblical Ethiopia was in the southern part of modern Egypt and was inhabited by Nubians, a tall, warlike black people.

Until fairly modern times everyone read out loud. Accordingly, it was an easy matter for Philip to know what the Ethiopian eunuch was reading when he drew near his chariot. Why do you think Philip asked the eunuch if he under- stood what he was reading? (Acts 8:30)

. . . .

. . . .

Why did the passage from Isaiah 53:7–8 make such an ideal launching pad for a presentation of the gospel of Jesus? (Acts 8:31–35)

. . . .

. . . .

CONSIDER THIS

Read the WILSB feature "The Message Spreads to Africa" (Acts 8:37-39). The Ethiopian eunuch "responded warmly to Philip and the message about Christ, and became the first known witness—black or white—to Africa. For the second time in Acts 8, the gospel moved outside of the narrow confines of Jerusalem and Judea."

The Old Testament law excluded eunuchs from the assembly of Israel (Deut. 23:1). But Isaiah had predicted that eunuchs would be welcome in the messianic kingdom (Is. 56:3–5). How does this help explain the eunuch's eagerness to believe and be baptized?

. . . .

. . . .

Who are people on the fringes of acceptability around you with whom you need to consider sharing the gospel of Christ?

. . . .

. . . .

◆ ◆ ◆ ◆ ◆ ◆ ◆ ◆

◆ THE PASSIONATE PERSECUTOR ◆
(Acts 9:1–19)

It was amazing that the gospel of Christ could leap the hostile ethnic hurdle between Jews and Samaritans. It was more startling that the gospel was able to breach the racial barrier between Jews and Gentiles—even through a proselyte or God fearer. Perhaps the greatest wonder of these chapters in Acts is that the good news of Jesus Christ could tame the raging spirit of a religious fanatic.

When Saul felt he had hounded the last Hellenistic Jewish believer in Jesus from Jerusalem, he set his sights on the city with the next largest population of Hellenistic Jews—Damascus. With extradition letters from the high priest in his possession, Saul took a posse and headed north northeast to the capital of Syria.

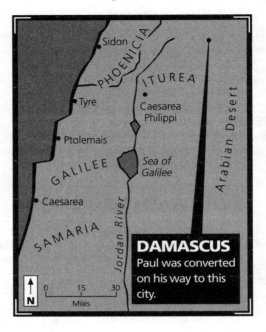

DAMASCUS
Paul was converted on his way to this city.

What were Saul's goals as a persecutor of followers of the Way? (Acts 9:1–2)

....

....

While the glory of God shone around Saul, the voice of Jesus addressed him three times. What do you think Jesus wanted Saul to realize as a result of each of these communications?

◆ Acts 9:4

....

....

◆ Acts 9:5

....

....

◆ Acts 9:6

....

....

What do you think Saul's two questions of the Lord reveal about his state of mind? (Acts 9:5–6)

. . . .

. . . .

What do you think Saul's traveling companions thought about this experience and its immediate effects on Saul? (Acts 9:7–8)

. . . .

. . . .

What spiritual issues do you think Saul reviewed during his three days of fasting and blindness? (Acts 9:9)

. . . .

. . . .

◆ ◆ ◆ ◆ ◆ ◆ ◆ ◆

💡 CONSIDER THIS

Read the *WILSB* features "Ananias—Scared But Obedient" (Acts 9:10–18) and "A Radically Changed Perception" (Acts 9:15). "Do you harbor deep doubts about certain people, convinced that they will never change, never enter the faith? In light of Ananias's experience, perhaps it's time to review your perspective."

What information from the Lord do you think gave Ananias the courage to go and confront Saul, the feared persecutor of believers in Jesus? (Acts 9:11–12, 15–16)

. . . .

. . . .

What do you think each part of Ananias's message would have meant to Saul? (Acts 9:17)

◆ "Brother Saul"

. . . .

. . . .

◆ "The Lord Jesus, who appeared to you . . . has sent me"

. . . .

. . . .

◆ "Receive your sight"

. . . .

. . . .

◆ "Be filled with the Holy Spirit"

. . . .

. . . .

Who's the most obstinate, antagonistic non-Christian you know?

. . . .

. . . .

How should you pray for that person in light of the example of Saul and Ananias?

. . . .

. . . .

◆ ◆ ◆ ◆ ◆ ◆ ◆ ◆

——— ◆ SAUL: TOO HOT TO HANDLE ◆ ———
(Acts 9:20–31)

What would it mean to the Jewish faithful and to the followers of Jesus that Saul had left orthodox Judaism and accepted Jesus as the Messiah and his personal Savior? Would Saul influence his former friends in high places to accept the Way? Saul had been an ardent promoter of Judaism. What sort of witness for Jesus would he be?

After his conversion, what was Saul's approach to sharing his new faith? (Acts 9:20, 22)

. . . .

. . . .

What was the initial reaction of the Jewish community to Saul's proclamation of the gospel of Christ? (Acts 9:21)

. . . .

. . . .

What was the eventual reaction of the Jewish community to Saul's successful apologetic for Jesus the Messiah? (Acts 9:23)

. . . .

. . . .

How did Saul escape the plot to kill him in Damascus? (Acts 9:24–25)

. . . .

. . . .

◆ ◆ ◆ ◆ ◆ ◆ ◆ ◆

◯ CONSIDER THIS

Read the *WILSB* feature "An Amplifier for the Gospel" (Acts 9:2–25). "Damascus turned out to be an important city in the life of the church. . . . A Christian church can still be found in Damascus—on a street called Straight."

Because major trade routes crossed in Damascus, merchants and travelers carried Christianity from the city for centuries along with their cargoes and moneybags. How did Damascus help the early church establish itself? (Acts 8:1, 4; 9:1–2, 23-25; Galatians 1:17–18)

. . . .

. . . .

What city or town have you seen be an "amplifier" of the gospel for its surrounding region? How did it do that?

. . . .

. . . .

Saul fled from Damascus to Jerusalem. When he arrived, what kind of reception did he receive from the community of believers in Jesus? (Acts 9:26)

. . . .

. . . .

◆ ◆ ◆ ◆ ◆ ◆ ◆ ◆

◯ CONSIDER THIS

Read the *WILSB* feature "Discipleship—Or Mentoring" (Acts 9:26-30). "Closely related to the making of disciples is the mentoring of leaders. . . . A mentor, then, is a trusted counselor or guide—typically an older, more experienced person who imparts valuable wisdom to someone younger."

How did Barnabas act as mentor for Saul among the Jerusalem believers? (Acts 9:26-28)

. . . .

. . . .

Who has served as a mentor for you and recommended you to others?

. . . .

. . . .

Who can you mentor and assist in Christian leadership by means of your recommendation and guidance?

. . . .

. . . .

When the Hellenistic Jews of Jerusalem planned to kill Saul (just as they had done in Damascus), the disciples sent him away to his hometown of Tarsus (Acts 9:29–30). Does this strike you as cowardly or wise? Why do you think so?

. . . .

. . . .

Jerusalem was unready to accept followers of Jesus who were anything other than Palestinian Jews who observed the temple ritual. But churches were growing in other areas of Palestine that understood the gospel more inclusively. What was happening in the churches throughout Jerusalem, all Judea, and Samaria? (Acts 1:8; 9:31)

. . . .

. . . .

Rate your church from 1 to 10 (10 is best) in each of the characteristics mentioned in Acts 9:31 by circling the appropriate number.

◆ Peace

| 1 | 2 | 3 | 4 | 5 | 6 | 7 | 8 | 9 | 10 |

◆ Edification

| 1 | 2 | 3 | 4 | 5 | 6 | 7 | 8 | 9 | 10 |

◆ Fear of the Lord

| 1 | 2 | 3 | 4 | 5 | 6 | 7 | 8 | 9 | 10 |

◆ Comfort of the Spirit

| 1 | 2 | 3 | 4 | 5 | 6 | 7 | 8 | 9 | 10 |

What characteristics of your church would you like to see strengthened? How do you think you could contribute to the strengthening of your church in these areas?

. . . .

. . . .

"GOD DON'T MAKE NO JUNK"

Acts 9:32—11:18

It was a bumper sticker and T-shirt slogan of the Jesus People era. It was an early version of the cry "I Am Somebody!" only it pointed out on what basis that's true. Ministries in urban centers found it spoke to young people who felt rejected, abused, and "thrown away" by families and society in general.

"God Don't Make No Junk!" The logic of the slogan was much better than its grammar—if you're a poor, urban teenager, made in the image of God, you aren't junk, even if you have been tossed around and discarded by foolish adults. Don't let anybody take away your self-esteem by the way they treat you. Look to God as the source of your value. He made you, and He don't make junk.

The first believers in Jesus—Palestinian Jews from Galilee and Judea—had been trained all their lives to regard non-Jews as junk. They struggled to treat Jews born outside of Palestine as first-class people (Acts 6:1). Gentiles were contaminants to be avoided.

No wonder Peter was surprised when the Lord led him away from Jerusalem to the outer edge of Palestine and ordered him to get involved with a Gentile eyeball to eyeball. Could Peter accept the notion that "God Don't Make No Junk"?

◆ ◆ ◆ ◆ ◆ ◆ ◆ ◆

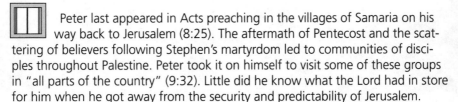

——— ◆ AWAY FROM HOME ◆ ———
(Acts 9:32–43)

Peter last appeared in Acts preaching in the villages of Samaria on his way back to Jerusalem (8:25). The aftermath of Pentecost and the scattering of believers following Stephen's martyrdom led to communities of disciples throughout Palestine. Peter took it on himself to visit some of these groups in "all parts of the country" (9:32). Little did he know what the Lord had in store for him when he got away from the security and predictability of Jerusalem.

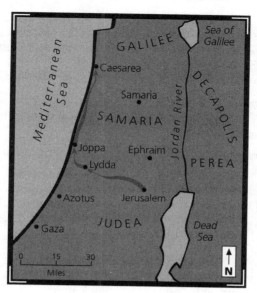

Lydda was a smallish town on the crossroads of two major highways. It was known as a center of rabbinic scholarship. What do you think it meant to the small community of believers in Jesus to be visited by Peter and have him work a great miracle there? (Acts 9:32–35)

. . . .

. . . .

Compare the healing of Aeneas (Acts 9:33–35) with the earlier healing of the lame man at the temple (3:2–10). What do these incidents reveal about Peter's understanding of how miracles occur?

. . . .

. . . .

Sharon (Acts 9:35) was the coastal plain that ran from Joppa to Mount Carmel on the point of land that juts out into the Mediterranean Sea north of Caesarea. How did the Lord arrange to get Peter from Lydda to Joppa on the plain of Sharon? (Acts 9:35–38)

. . . .

. . . .

Tabitha and Dorcas (both meant "gazelle") were the Hebrew and Greek names of a Hellenistic Jewess who had died in Joppa. When Peter raised Dorcas from the dead, he behaved very much as Jesus had when He raised Jairus's daughter from the dead (see Mark 5:40–43). Why do you think Luke included the healing of Aeneas and the resurrection of Dorcas by Peter just before he was summoned to share the gospel with Gentiles?

Circle the letter of the explanation that doesn't fit the evidence.

a. The power of the Spirit of God expressed itself more and more mightily as Peter moved farther away from Jerusalem into areas where Jews and Gentiles mixed.

b. The gospel was preceding the apostles into the towns and villages of Palestine. It could not be contained.

c. The gospel quickly united believers into caring, witnessing groups, united by the power of God's Spirit.

d. When Peter was most like Jesus in power and compassion, he was ready to accept the biggest challenge of his ministry—taking the gospel to the Gentiles.

e. Peter was getting proud of his power and authority, so the Lord used the situation with Cornelius to humble him.

Joppa was a seaport (modern Jaffa) that served Jerusalem's modest shipping needs. Since tanners handled skins and animal carcasses, Simon, Peter's host in Joppa, would regularly have been ceremonially unclean and excluded from Jewish worship. Peter's willingness to stay with Simon showed indifference to some of the pickier aspects of Jewish traditions. What happened as a result of Peter's healing and teaching ministries in Lydda and Joppa? (Acts 9:35, 42)

. . . .

. . . .

Some people relish new situations and challenges. Others prefer the familiar and secure. On the following scale, rate your attitude toward situations you don't feel totally prepared for.

1	2	3	4	5	6	7	8	9	10
SCARED SPITLESS		RELUCTANT HERO				WILLING WARRIOR		CHOMPING AT THE BIT	

How is the Lord pulling you away from your comfort zone into areas of life where you may face new challenges? What do you think those challenges may be?

. . . .

. . . .

◆ ◆ ◆ ◆ ◆ ◆ ◆ ◆

◆ A DIVINE APPOINTMENT ◆
(Acts 10:1–23)

It's comforting to know that God carefully prepares His people for the experiences that will change their lives forever. At the time it may not seem as though He has given any warning or advance information about the pivotal event. Usually that means we didn't understand His preparation and it's up to hindsight to spot all of the signposts and information packets the Lord had put along the way. Notice how puzzled Peter was by perfectly good advice until he was in the middle of a date with destiny.

Herod the Great had built the artificial harbor and beautiful city of Caesarea because he was angry with the residents of Joppa. Caesarea had replaced Joppa as the major Mediterranean port for Judea and become the Roman administrative capital for the province. Cornelius and his Italian Regiment were crack troops from the Italian peninsula attached to the governor's personal service.

◆ ◆ ◆ ◆ ◆ ◆ ◆ ◆

✔ FOR YOUR INFO

Read the *Word in Life Study Bible (WILSB)* feature "Personality Profile: Cornelius" (Acts 10:1). Compare the character of Dorcas, the believer in Christ, with that of Cornelius, the Gentile who was curious about Judaism. (Acts 9:36, 39; 10:2)

. . . .

. . . .

Cornelius was "a devout man and one who feared God" (Acts 10:2). He probably wasn't a God fearer as the Ethiopian eunuch was (8:27), because his conversion was regarded as the salvation of a full Gentile. How do you know from Acts 10:3–6 that Cornelius had a spiritual hunger?

. . . .

. . . .

How do you think God might respond to unbelievers around the world today who find they have a desire to know Him?

. . . .

. . . .

What was the point of Peter's vision of the sheet filled with all the animals? (Acts 10:9–16)

. . . .

. . . .

Why do you think the Lord repeated the vision three times? (Acts 10:16)

. . . .

. . . .

Philip was living in Caesarea at the time (Acts 8:40) and had experience evangelizing Gentiles (vv. 26–39). Why do you think the Lord wanted Peter—not Philip—to be the one who shared the gospel with Cornelius?

. . . .

. . . .

When Peter heard about Cornelius and the angel (Acts 10:22), what do you think he began to understand about his own vision?

. . . .

. . . .

It is to the credit of Peter and Simon the tanner that they gave overnight lodgings to Cornelius's servants and their escort. Jews did not typically share housing and meals with Gentiles. The soldier was a Gentile, and the servants may have been too.

When has the gospel put you in intimate contact with people you ordinarily would have little to do with?

. . . .

. . . .

What did you learn from that situation?

. . . .

. . . .

◆ ◆ ◆ ◆ ◆ ◆ ◆ ◆

—— ◆ THE OUTSIDERS ARE IN ◆ ——
(Acts 10:24–48)

There are a few pivotal moments in the life of the entire church, individual congregations, and individual Christians when God intervenes and exercises unusual control. Peter experienced one of those rare moments when he arrived in Caesarea and entered the home of Cornelius the centurion. A page was turning in human history. There would be no going back to the old ways because God had turned that page.

What things did Peter feel he needed to make clear to Cornelius upon arrival at his house? (Acts 10:24–29)

. . . .

. . . .

What did Cornelius expect as a result of the angelic message and Peter's arrival? (Acts 10:30–33)

. . . .

. . . .

Roman military personnel were forbidden to marry,[1] so Cornelius's "household" (Acts 10:2) and "relatives" (v. 24) refer to servants and fellow countrymen (other soldiers) rather than to a wife and children. How does Cornelius's interest in his servants and fellow countrymen fit in with the other things said about him?

. . . .

. . . .

Cornelius could show humility by bowing before Peter (Acts 10:25) and an air of authority by assuring Peter he had done the right thing in answering his summons (v. 33). Peter resisted the flattery of inappropriate worship (v. 26), and he took no offense at Cornelius's authoritative ways. Which troubles you more in dealing with people: flattery or authority? Why?

. . . .

. . . .

If you were called on to share the gospel with a powerful nonbeliever from a corporation, political party, or social group you strongly disliked, which of the following responses best represents the way you would react?

a. Anger because you would have to deal with a person you disapproved of.

b. Fear that you wouldn't represent the gospel of Christ well.

c. Suspicion that this person really wanted to discredit the gospel rather than believe it.

d. Excitement about the chance to share Christ with someone discerning, motivated, and influential.

e. Pride that you were the one who got to deal with an important person

f. Other

. . . .

. . . .

Circle the letters of the following situations in which you have witnessed for Christ. Then draw a box around the ones you would rather not face. Finally, put a star by the boxed situation that would be most difficult for you.

a. A family member

b. A neighbor

c. A school friend

d. A fellow worker

e. A church visitation contact

f. On a mission trip

g. After a church service

h. With a homeless person

i. Across the African-American/Anglo barrier

j. With a welfare mother

k. Across the Hispanic/Anglo barrier

l. Across the Asian/Anglo barrier

m. With a secular humanist

n. With a mass murderer

o. With a sex offender against children

p. With a Muslim fundamentalist

When Peter said that God accepts "whoever fears Him and works righteousness" (Acts 10:34), he did not use "accept" as a synonym for "save." What "acceptance" had Cornelius's reverence and righteousness gained him up to that point?

. . . .

. . . .

Summarize the message of Peter about Jesus in one sentence of no more than 30 words. (Acts 10:34–43)

. . . .

. . . .

CONSIDER THIS

Read the *WILSB* feature "Ethnic Walls Break Down" (Acts 10:44–45). "When Peter met Cornelius—an officer of Rome's occupation troops in Palestine—two conversions took place: Cornelius, his family, and his friends came to faith; and Peter came to realize that God wants Gentiles in the church."

In Peter's eyes, how many facts about Cornelius, recorded or implied in Acts 10, made him objectionable?

. . . .

. . . .

In God's eyes, how many facts about Cornelius, recorded or implied in Acts 10, moved God to send Peter to him?

. . . .

. . . .

What did Peter learn about God's intentions toward the Gentiles through his contact with Cornelius? (Acts 10:34–35, 44–48)

. . . .

. . . .

How has God changed your attitudes toward people of other races?

. . . .

. . . .

What further changes in your racial attitudes do you think He might expect of you in the future?

. . . .

. . . .

◆ ◆ ◆ ◆ ◆ ◆ ◆ ◆

◆ "IF I HADN'T SEEN IT, I WOULDN'T HAVE BELIEVED IT" ◆
(Acts 11:1–18)

God had arranged for Cornelius and Peter to meet. The divine element was undeniable. He saw to it that six Jewish witnesses accompanied Peter to Cornelius's house to verify everything that happened (Acts 11:12). Finally, He poured out the Holy Spirit on Cornelius and his guests as indisputable evidence that believing Gentiles were fully in His grace (10:44, 47). Even so, it was difficult for Peter to convince the Jewish believers in Jerusalem that his mission to Cornelius had been of God's doing.

The Jewish believers were not concerned that the Gentiles had believed in Jesus as their Savior. What did bother them? (Acts 11:1–3)

. . . .

. . . .

Today, also, biased Christians welcome the salvation of people they don't like while objecting to social contact with them. What kinds of social contacts with other races do prejudiced Christians often object to?

. . . .

. . . .

How does the significance of Peter's vision apply to the objection of biased Christians to social contacts with people of other races? (Acts 11:4–9)

. . . .

. . . .

Peter didn't focus on explaining his social contacts with Cornelius and his household and friends. Instead he focused on the legitimacy of their conversion and reception of the Holy Spirit (Acts 11:15–17). What were the implications for the Jewish social biases against Gentiles that the Gentiles became Christians just as they had?

. . . .

. . . .

What are the implications for biased Christians today that the objects of their prejudices become Christians just as they do?

. . . .

. . . .

There were two stages to the response of the Jewish believers in Jerusalem (Acts 11:18). What do you think was happening to their biases during each of them?

◆ Silence

. . . .

. . . .

◆ Glorifying God

. . . .

. . . .

CONSIDER THIS

Read the *WILSB* feature "Come One, Come All!" (Acts 10:34). "Luke peppers his Acts account with incidents of ethnic tension and prejudice, and also their resolution in Christ." Read the following excerpts from Acts and indicate the ethnic barrier Jesus overcame.

◆ Acts 6:1–7

. . . .

. . . .

◆ Acts 8:5–8

. . . .
. . . .

◆ Acts 8:26–40

. . . .
. . . .

◆ Acts 10:1–48

. . . .
. . . .

◆ Acts 11:19–26

. . . .
. . . .

◆ Acts 13:1—14:26

. . . .
. . . .

◆ Acts 15:1-33

. . . .
. . . .

1. Craig S. Keener, *The IVP Bible Background Commentary: New Testament* (Downers Grove, IL: InterVarsity Press, 1993), 350.

THE WITNESS SPREADS
FAR AND WIDE

Acts 11:19—20:38

In this portion of Acts, the gospel of Jesus Christ rippled out to the major cities of the eastern Mediterranean world. Neither Jerusalem nor Caesarea but Antioch of Syria became the center of evangelistic outreach for the young church. The mother church in Jerusalem would be the watchdog to ensure the purity of Christian expansion, but the impetus for growth was felt in Gentile areas.

The key cities of Asia Minor and Greece stirred with Christian activity. By the end of Acts 20, only Rome awaited a visit from the apostle Paul before the Roman world had been penetrated by the gospel. There could be no doubt that Rome would surrender to Jesus too.

THE POT STARTS TO BOIL

Acts 11:19—13:12

The people of the little church had worshiped together for many years. They were friendly and loving to one another. They operated a quality Sunday school for children and young people. The missions program generously supported a group of fine missionaries around the world. The building was tidy and bright.

Then a new pastor replaced the familiar shepherd who moved on to another congregation in a larger community. Soon it was clear that things were going to change. The new pastor was energetic and filled with new ideas. Some members of the church were excited about the possibilities of outreach and expansion. Others feared that changes might disrupt the familiar patterns that had served the church so well for so long.

One thing was clear. Something was going to happen. The church was like a pot of water sitting on the burner of a stove. Little wisps of steam were rising now and then from the surface. Bubbles were collecting on the sides of the pot below the water line. It was about to boil. Something was going to happen. Hopefully it would be something good.

As the gospel of Jesus surged in ever-widening ripples away from Jerusalem, it became increasingly obvious that something was about to happen. The familiar Jewish patterns that fit Jerusalem so well didn't fit the cities with mixed Jewish-Gentile populations. The pot was about to boil.

◆ ◆ ◆ ◆ ◆ ◆ ◆ ◆

——— ◆ ANTIOCH TAKES THE LEAD ◆ ———

(Acts 11:19–30)

Antioch was the third city of the Roman Empire, behind Rome and Alexandria. Its population exceeded 500,000. It was divided into walled quarters for Greek, Syrian, African, and Jewish residents. God chose Antioch as His laboratory for experiments with a church that could unite diverse people into a loving, serving community of faith in Jesus.

69

What were the outer limits of the gospel expansion propelled by the martyrdom of Stephen? (Acts 11:19)

. . . .

. . . .

In earlier references, Luke used the term Hellenist to refer to Jews raised in a Greek culture (Acts 6:1; 9:29). In 11:20 Luke contrasted "Hellenists" with "Jews only" to mean Gentiles. Who took the daring step of proclaiming the gospel to Gentiles in Antioch and what happened when they did? (Acts 11:19)

. . . .

. . . .

It's still likely that these Gentiles had some connection to Judaism, as the Ethiopian eunuch and Cornelius did, because this situation did not create as great a furor as did Paul's later outreach to true pagans in pagan settings. Nonetheless, what happened when the mother church in Jerusalem heard about strange goings-on in Antioch? (Acts 11:22–24)

. . . .

. . . .

What was the reaction of Barnabas to the Jewish-Gentile church in Antioch? (Acts 11:23–26; see 9:26–30)

. . . .

. . . .

CONSIDER THIS

Read the *Word in Life Study Bible (WILSB)* feature "Churches—Keys to the Cities" (Acts 11:22). "Christianity eventually prevailed as the dominant worldview and social force in the Roman world. One reason: it planted churches in dozens of the empire's major cities by the end of the first century."

How do you think the churches in your community could unite to express firm but loving Christian responses to the major social issues of the day?

. . . .

. . . .

How do you think churches and Christians need to adjust their behavior as Christianity becomes a minority view in your community?

. . . .

. . . .

What advantages and disadvantages are there for Christians as a minority group in influencing our culture?

. . . .

. . . .

◆ ◆ ◆ ◆ ◆ ◆ ◆ ◆

CONSIDER THIS

Read the *WILSB* feature "A New Reality Gets Its Name" (Acts 11:26). "Are there perceptions of the faith where you live and work that are inadequate? Can you change some of those with a display of what following Christ actually involves?"

What was happening in the church of Antioch that prompted onlookers to attach the new name "Christian" to the group? (Acts 11:20–26).

. . . .

. . . .

What qualities or behaviors do you think believers need to show unbelievers to deserve the label Christian?

. . . .

. . . .

How did the adventurous church at Antioch show its solidarity with the cautious mother church in Jerusalem? (Acts 11:27–30)

. . . .

. . . .

◆ ◆ ◆ ◆ ◆ ◆ ◆ ◆

——— ◆ TROUBLE THREATENS IN ◆ ———
JERUSALEM
(Acts 12:1–11)

While the church in Antioch operated in an expansion mode, the church in Jerusalem found itself forced more and more into a survival mode. It's easy to imagine how a fortress mentality began to grow in the Jerusalem church. In this situation, the bad guy was Herod Agrippa I, a grandson of Herod the Great who ruled when Jesus was born and a nephew to Herod Antipas who executed John the Baptist and concurred in Jesus' death.

Herod Agrippa I was half Jewish, and he worked hard all during his administration to curry favor with the Jewish leaders. What new approach to acceptability with the power structure of Judea did Herod discover during the time scattering witnesses were taking the gospel to Phoenicia, Cyprus, and Antioch? (Acts 12:1–4)

. . . .

. . . .

Peter probably was held in the fortress of Antonia the Romans had built adjacent to the temple complex. Identify all of the layers of security you can detect in the account of Peter's release. (Acts 12:4–10)

. . . .

. . . .

Why do you think Luke stressed that Peter was too groggy to understand that his escape was really happening? (Acts 12:9, 11)

. . . .

. . . .

When James was imprisoned, God didn't intervene and he died. When Peter was imprisoned, an angel of God intervened very decisively (Acts 12:7–8) and he was saved. Surely the church prayed for James as well as for Peter (v. 5).

Circle the letter of the statement that best expresses the spiritual conclusion you would draw from this set of circumstances.

a. Political leaders are corrupt. Christians should avoid all involvements with politics and government.

b. The person who gets the most people praying for him or her has the best chance of being delivered from difficulties.

c. God isn't very fair or consistent in the way He treats those who believe in Him.

d. God delivers some of us from suffering; He delivers others of us through suffering.

e. God has favorites among Christians. I need to stay on His good side so He'll treat me well.

f. Other

. . . .

. . . .

❖ ❖ ❖ ❖ ❖ ❖ ❖ ❖

───── ❖   TROUBLE RESOLVED IN JERUSALEM   ❖ ─────
(Acts 12:12–24)

God had no intention of abandoning the church at Jerusalem. His Spirit and the gospel continued to influence many lives there, and God addressed the powerful foes who wanted to oppress the believers in Jesus. No opponents of the gospel of Christ, no matter how powerful, are ever secure because they have picked on the Creator and Ruler of all things.

What features of the text suggest that the praying Christians didn't expect a miraculous response from God to their petitions? (Acts 12:12–15)

. . . .

. . . .

Earlier, when Peter had been released from prison, the Lord sent him to the temple to preach (Acts 5:19–20). This time Peter went away to escape execution (12:17). What are some of the clues that tell you when to stay and witness in a hopeful situation and when to withdraw from a hopeless one?

. . . .

. . . .

73

What examples does the text of Acts give of the arbitrary and selfish nature of Herod's use of power? (Acts 12:18–23)

. . . .

. . . .

An angel of the Lord first struck Peter to rouse him (Acts 12:7) and then struck Herod to kill him (v. 23). The same power of God that blesses His children destroys His opponents. Why did the Lord take Herod's life? (Acts 12:1–3, 21–23)

. . . .

. . . .

As a result of Peter's angelic jailbreak and Herod's pride-intoxicated death, the Jerusalem church experienced a great spurt of growth based on the Word of God (Acts 12:24). When in your life has an expression of the power of God resulted in a time of great growth and confidence in Him?

. . . .

. . . .

What person or church that you care about needs a jolt of God's power to get them out of a survival mode into a growth mode? How could you pray for this person or church?

. . . .

. . . .

◆ ◆ ◆ ◆ ◆ ◆ ◆ ◆

◆ ANTIOCH SENDS MISSIONARIES ◆
(Acts 12:25—13:12)

While the cautious Jerusalem church experienced a burst of growth and confidence because of the Lord's powerful protection, the dynamic church at Antioch launched an initiative that finally would fulfill Jesus' command in Acts 1:8 to witness of Him to the ends of the earth.

When Barnabas and Saul returned from Jerusalem to Antioch following their famine relief mission (Acts 11:29–30), they took with them John Mark (12:25). John Mark was Barnabas's cousin (see Col. 4:10), the son of the hostess of the Jerusalem church (Acts 12:12), and probably a representative of the conservative views of the Jewish Christians of the mother church.

74

🌐 YOU ARE THERE

Read the *WILSB* feature "Antioch: A Model for the Modern Church" (Acts 13:1–3). "Even though first-century Christians made regular pilgrimages to Jerusalem and met annually in the upper room, the city of Antioch—not Jerusalem—was the center of early Christianity."

What can you gather about the ministry of the church at Antioch from the list of leaders in Acts 13:1?

. . . .
. . . .

Why do you think the Holy Spirit chose this church to be the basis of world evangelization? (Acts 13:3)

. . . .
. . . .

Why do you think the Spirit chose Barnabas and Saul, the key leaders of the church, to become the first missionary team?

. . . .
. . . .

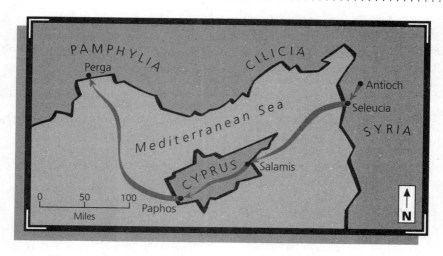

The touring evangelists started their ministry in Cyprus (Acts 13:4), the home territory of Barnabas (4:36), with some of the founders of the church at Antioch (11:2). What was the strategy of Barnabas and Saul there? (Acts 13:5)

. . . .
. . . .

Paphos was the Roman capital of Cyprus. Roman officials were responsible for approving or prohibiting the teaching of philosophies or religions in their territory. Elymas the sorcerer, who evidently represented Judaism—an approved creed—to the proconsul of Cyprus, opposed granting Barnabas and Saul official permission to proclaim the gospel of Christ. What happened when the proconsul decided to look into the gospel for himself? (Acts 13:6–12)

. . . .

. . . .

♀ CONSIDER THIS

Read the *WILSB* feature "Cyprus, a Geographic Hyphen" (Acts 13:4–12). "Cyprus was . . . a 'hyphen,' a bridge between East and West. As such, its coastal cities were frequently exposed to new ideas and influences, which they tended to adopt, much like coastal cities today."

How did Paul's encounter with Elymas the sorcerer illustrate the conflict he would have with Jewish authorities throughout his ministry? (Acts 13:9–11).

. . . .

. . . .

Through the book of Acts, the Jerusalem church operates increasingly in a survival mode. The Antioch church operates in an expansion mode. Do you approach your Christian life and witness in a survival mode or an expansion one? Rate yourself on the following scale.

1	2	3	4	5	6	7	8	9	10

SUPER-CAUTIOUS	QUIET BUT FIRM	READY TO WITNESS	FULL SPEED AHEAD

Does your church approach its ministry for the Lord in a survival mode or an expansion one? Rate your church on the following scale.

1	2	3	4	5	6	7	8	9	10

BARELY SURVIVING	NICE AND QUIET	HAVING AN IMPACT	THE TALK OF THE TOWN

What is something you would like to accomplish for the Lord in your lifetime? What can you do to prepare to meet this ambition?

. . . .

. . . .

"THE WALLS CAME ATUMBLIN' DOWN"

Acts 13:13—15:35

I n Ken Burns's *Story of Baseball, one of the shameful subplots is the racial segregation of the game before 1948. Early in the history of the sport, players of various racial groups earned spots on teams, but in hard times the majority resented losing any paying positions to minority groups. Soon all non-whites were unofficially barred from professional baseball by a "gentlemen's agreement" among team owners.*

Various groups formed their own teams, but none rivaled the black major leagues that competed with white teams for the dollars of black fans in most major midwestern cities. During World War II many black and white men experienced integration for the first time in the military. Many black soldiers had no interest in returning to the civilian world they had helped protect as less than full members of society.

Jackie Robinson was inevitable in post-World War II America. When Branch Rickey signed Robinson to play for the Brooklyn Dodgers, a hole had been poked in baseball's dam of segregation that quickly brought an end to the despicable "gentlemen's agreement." Robinson and other pioneers paid a tremendous personal price, but they brought the racial barriers tumbling down for African-American and Hispanic ball players.

In Acts parallel ministries emerged: a church of believing Jews and Jewish proselytes centered in Jerusalem and a church of believing Hellenistic Jews and Gentiles centered in Antioch. Would a "gentlemen's agreement" separate them into first- and second-class churches? Or would someone play Jackie Robinson to bring the walls tumbling down?

❖ ❖ ❖ ❖ ❖ ❖ ❖ ❖

───── ◆ EVERYBODY LOVES A STORY ◆ ─────
(Acts 13:13–41)

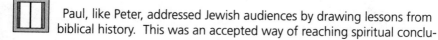

Paul, like Peter, addressed Jewish audiences by drawing lessons from biblical history. This was an accepted way of reaching spiritual conclusions in first-century rabbinic Judaism. Everybody loved *the* story of how God chose and nurtured a people for His name. Paul could enter any synagogue anywhere he went and tell the same story, knowing the Jews and God-fearing Gentiles in attendance would know what he was talking about.

◆ ◆ ◆ ◆ ◆ ◆ ◆ ◆

💡 CONSIDER THIS

Read the *Word in Life Study Bible (WILSB)* feature "Why Did John Mark Go Home?" (Acts 13:13). "Scripture doesn't tell us why John Mark made the decision to go home. But the encouraging thing is that his return didn't disqualify him from the faith or diminish his spirituality."

What happens to your opinion of yourself when you don't finish something you start?

. . . .

. . . .

What happens to your opinion of others when they don't finish what they start?

. . . .

. . . .

How should we look at our failures to benefit from them rather than be destroyed by them?

. . . .
. . . .

Antioch of Pisidia sat astride the Via Sebaste, a Roman road built by Augustus in 6 B.C., which linked the four cities featured in Acts 13 and 14: Antioch, Iconium, Lystra, and Derbe. How did Paul and Barnabas gain a hearing by the Jews of Pisidian Antioch? (Acts 13:14–15)

. . . .
. . . .

What were the two groups in Paul's synagogue audience? (Acts 13:16, 26)

. . . .
. . . .

What three points did Paul make from the Old Testament about God's relationship with Israel? (v. 17; vv. 18–19; vv. 20–22)

. . . .
. . . .

What four points did Paul make from the ministry of Jesus about God's relationship with Israel? (v. 23; vv. 24–25; vv. 27–29; vv. 30–31)

. . . .
. . . .

What did Paul establish about Jesus by quoting Psalm 2:7; Isaiah 55:3; and Psalm 16:10? (Acts 13:33–37)

. . . .
. . . .

What was Paul's appeal to the synagogue audience in Pisidian Antioch?

◆ Positively (Acts 13:38–39)

. . . .
. . . .

◆ Negatively (Acts 13:40–41)

. . . .
. . . .

───── ◆ **NOBODY LIKES A SORE LOSER** ◆ ─────
(Acts 13:42–52)

 When the Jewish authorities understood that Paul was preaching a justi-
fication for Jews and Gentiles through the death of Jesus Christ apart
from the Law of Moses (Acts 13:38–39), they were troubled. When they saw
their whole community fascinated by this message, they became fierce enemies
of the apostles. They eventually developed a campaign to have the message of
Jesus banned in every town in the region.

What was the initial response of various segments of the synagogue
audience in Pisidian Antioch to the gospel of Jesus Christ? (Acts 13:42–43)

. . . .

. . . .

Why did the Jewish authorities finally decide to oppose the message of
Paul, and how did they do it? (Acts 13:44–45)

. . . .

. . . .

What reasons did Paul and Barnabas give their Jewish opponents for
turning from them to the Gentiles as the target audience of their witness? (Acts
13:46–48)

. . . .

. . . .

What were the results of Paul and Barnabas's ministry to the Gentiles in
Pisidian Antioch? (Acts 13:48–52)

. . . .

. . . .

───── ◆ **A STEP AHEAD OF THE MOB** ◆ ─────
(Acts 14:1–27)

 Since each community had its own local government, Paul and Barnabas
figured moving east along the Via Sebaste to the next town gave them a
fresh start once they wore out their welcome in the previous one. As the opposition got organized, they sent envoys after the apostles to alert the local
authorities that Paul and Barnabas were trouble-makers. The apostles had to
work fast.

80

What were the dynamics of the interaction between Paul and Barnabas, the Jews, and the Gentiles during the extended ministry in Iconium? (Acts 14:1–3)

. . . .

. . . .

What were the outcomes of the ministry of Paul and Barnabas in Iconium? (Acts 14:4–7)

. . . .

. . . .

In Lystra, the next town along the Roman highway, Paul healed a lame man in an encounter similar to an earlier healing by Peter in the temple in Jerusalem (Acts 3:1–7). What was the response of the local population to Paul's healing of the lame man? (Acts 14:11–13)

. . . .

. . . .

◆ ◆ ◆ ◆ ◆ ◆ ◆ ◆

CONSIDER THIS

Read the _WILSB_ feature "Confusing Responses" (Acts 14:11–19). "The good news can either raise a person's hopes or strike fear at levels that are hard to perceive. That's why believers today need to be ready for extreme reactions when they present the gospel."

Why were there such radically different first responses to the gospel in Iconium (Acts 14:1–2) and in Lystra (vv. 11–13)?

. . . .

. . . .

What help can you anticipate from the Lord in dealing with unexpected strong reactions to a non-offensive presentation of the good news of Jesus Christ?

. . . .

. . . .

When Barnabas and Paul finally understood that the natives of Lystra intended to worship them as gods, they did everything possible to stop them (Acts 14:14, 18). How did they reason from nature that there is a "living God" superior to all so-called "gods"? (Acts 13:15–17)

. . . .

. . . .

Circle the letter of the reason that you think best explains why the Lystrans who had wanted to worship Barnabas and Paul were so easily convinced by the delegation from Pisidian Antioch and Iconium to stone Paul (Acts 14:19).

a. They wanted to see if Paul really was a god who couldn't be hurt by stones.

b. The apostles had offended a lot of people by trying to correct a popular superstition and teach about a moral God who expects things of them.

c. The Lystrans respected and admired the highly ethical Jews of Antioch and Iconium, so they did whatever the Jews wanted.

d. Gentiles hated all Jews, so the Lystrans took any opportunity to alienate one group of Jews from another.

e. Mob action is fickle. Impulsive worship and impulsive violence are not far apart in motivation.

Timothy came from Lystra and joined Paul on his second missionary expedition (Acts 16:1–2). What do you imagine it meant to Timothy through his years of travel and ministry with Paul to be able to recall Paul rising from the dead after being stoned in Lystra and walking off toward Derbe the next day to preach some more? (Acts 14:20)

. . . .

. . . .

It took a lot of courage for Paul and Barnabas to revisit every city which had expelled them. Why did they take such a risk? (Acts 14:21–23)

. . . .

. . . .

Paul and Barnabas reported in detail about their mission to the church in Antioch (Acts 14:26–28). Circle the letter of the statement that best reflects your attitude toward being accountable to a spiritual authority.

a. I'm part of the body of Christ that sends me out to serve the Lord. They are a part of everything I do, so I should share that ministry with them in detail.

b. Knowing I'll have to make detailed reports about my work keeps me on my toes so I perform my very best.

c. I believe I'm accountable to no one but God for the Christian service I perform.

d. Keeping the sending church happy is the best way to keep financial and prayer support coming in.

e. It's very encouraging and inspiring for people to hear about the experiences of missionaries in foreign lands.

◆ ◆ ◆ ◆ ◆ ◆ ◆ ◆

—— ◆ "WHAT GOD HAS JOINED ◆ ——
TOGETHER . . ."
(Acts 15:1–21)

When Cornelius became a believer in Jesus, he didn't establish a pattern of Gentile conversions. When the church at Antioch included Gentile members, they still had some sort of relationship to Judaism first. But when Paul and Barnabas established churches in Asia Minor that included pure pagan Gentile believers, the mother church in Jerusalem could not ignore the revolutionary implications of Christian faith that had no connection to the Law of Moses.

How did the argument develop that had to be settled by the council at Jerusalem? (Acts 15:1–2)

. . . .

. . . .

How did this argument divide the existing churches? (Acts 15:3–5)

. . . .

. . . .

◆ ◆ ◆ ◆ ◆ ◆ ◆ ◆

CONSIDER THIS

Read the *WILSB* features "Growth Leads to New Understanding" (Acts 15:2) and "Issues of Faith and Culture" (Acts 15:6). "An encounter with a different culture can sometimes force believers to evaluate what they believe and why."

What are some "truth issues"—matters of doctrine and biblical interpretation—that people differ over in your church?

. . . .

. . . .

What are some "love issues"—matters of open-mindedness and toleration—that people differ over in your church?

. . . .

. . . .

◆ ◆ ◆ ◆ ◆ ◆ ◆ ◆

CONSIDER THIS

Read the *WILSB* feature "Sure You're Saved . . . Sort of" (Acts 15:1–21). "Even in the church we often find our security in sameness and sometimes exclude those who differ. Diversity feels uncomfortable. But in Acts 15, we might consider what it would take to address our concerns honestly and biblically."

What role did Peter's testimony play in the conclusion of the Jerusalem council? (Acts 15:7–11)

. . . .

. . . .

What part did the report of Barnabas and Paul play in the decision of the Jerusalem council? (Acts 15:12)

. . . .

. . . .

What contribution to the decision of the Jerusalem council did James the brother of Jesus make by referring to Amos 9:11–12? (Acts 15:13–21)

. . . .

. . . .

On the following scales circle the numbers that represent the actual strength of each component in resolving differences in your church. Then put a box around the number in each scale that represents the strength you think each component should have in resolving differences.

SOCIETAL NORMS

1	2	3	4	5	6	7	8	9	10

THE OPINIONS OF LEADERS

1	2	3	4	5	6	7	8	9	10

BIBLICAL THEOLOGY

1	2	3	4	5	6	7	8	9	10

◆ ── "... LET NOT MAN PUT ASUNDER" ◆ ──
(Acts 15:22–35)

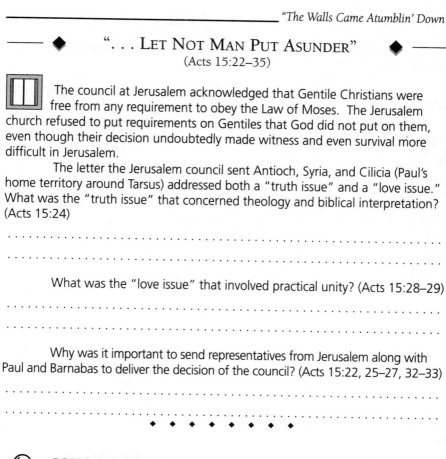

The council at Jerusalem acknowledged that Gentile Christians were free from any requirement to obey the Law of Moses. The Jerusalem church refused to put requirements on Gentiles that God did not put on them, even though their decision undoubtedly made witness and even survival more difficult in Jerusalem.

The letter the Jerusalem council sent Antioch, Syria, and Cilicia (Paul's home territory around Tarsus) addressed both a "truth issue" and a "love issue." What was the "truth issue" that concerned theology and biblical interpretation? (Acts 15:24)

. . . .

. . . .

What was the "love issue" that involved practical unity? (Acts 15:28–29)

. . . .

. . . .

Why was it important to send representatives from Jerusalem along with Paul and Barnabas to deliver the decision of the council? (Acts 15:22, 25–27, 32–33)

. . . .

. . . .

◆ ◆ ◆ ◆ ◆ ◆ ◆

○ CONSIDER THIS

Read the *WILSB* feature "A Church That Defies Market Research" (Acts 15:22–35). "As the twentieth century closes and the twenty-first century begins, the population of the United States is becoming increasingly diverse. Can the church prosper in a pluralistic society? Yes, judging by Acts."

What conclusions would you draw from the first fifteen chapters of Acts about the importance or desirability of diversity in the church of Jesus Christ?

. . . .

. . . .

What do the first fifteen chapters of Acts suggest are the strengths and weaknesses of a church composed of people from just one background?

. . . .

. . . .

What kinds of conflicts does the first half of Acts suggest that a diverse church can expect to face?

. . . .

. . . .

What sorts of spiritual gains does the first half of Acts suggest that a diverse church will make if it struggles and solves its conflicts?

. . . .

. . . .

Write a prayer for your church in which you ask God to bless your church as it deals with the "culture clashes" it has to deal with.

. . . .

. . . .

"TO BOLDLY GO WHERE NO MAN HAS GONE BEFORE"

Acts 15:36—17:34

*I**n 1901, the story goes, a nineteen-year-old cowhand from the Triple X
Ranch liked to watch the bats swirl like a tornado every evening out of the
mouth of a cave in the desert. One night he used his knotted lariat to
inch 200 feet into the darkness to the edge of a drop-off. To the amusement
of the other cowpokes in the bunkhouse, Jim made a ladder of rope with
mesquite and juniper rungs to find out what was below that cliff.*

With his ladder, a lantern, and a can of kerosene, Jim White dropped into the darkness of his cave. At first he wandered through waist-deep drifts of musty bat guano. Then he pushed on into a chamber that stretched on and on before it too dropped into a stupendous pit whose size he couldn't estimate in the glow of his little light.

With the help of a Mexican boy he called Pothead, Jim White used all his spare time to explore an unfolding maze of caverns that seemed to have no end. After some time Jim and Pothead found what they called the Big Room, a chamber 4,000 feet long, 600 feet wide, and 250 feet high.

It took twenty years for the scattered local citizens to get interested in Jim White's cave. Then it only took ten more years to turn it into a favorite national park named after the nearest large town of Carlsbad, New Mexico.[1]

*The Carlsbad Caverns story is at least part legend, but Acts is sober
history. It records the groundbreaking venture of Paul and Silas into territory
where no one had ever taken the gospel of Jesus Christ. Whereas Jim
White's pioneering changed the face of spelunking in America, Paul and
Silas' pioneering changed the spiritual history of the world.*

❖ ❖ ❖ ❖ ❖ ❖ ❖ ❖

───── ◆   FINDING A NEW FRONTIER   ◆ ─────
(Acts 15:36—16:10)

Paul did not leave Antioch of Syria in search of a new frontier. He set out to strengthen and encourage the churches already established in earlier ministries. Paul was doing in person what his epistles would do later. Fortunately, "the missionary journeys of Paul reveal an extraordinary combination of strategic planning and sensitivity to the guidance of the Holy Spirit in working out the details of the main goals."[2] Paul never seemed to mind when the Lord pointed him in new directions.

◆ ◆ ◆ ◆ ◆ ◆ ◆ ◆

♀ CONSIDER THIS

Read the *Word in Life Study Bible (WILSB)* feature "The Tension Between Truth and Love" (Acts 15:39). "Are there times when your commitment to doctrinal truth causes you to forget that no matter how right or wrong others may be, they are people who need to be loved?"

How would you describe the disagreement between Paul and Barnabas over the role of John Mark in their ministry? (Acts 15:36–38).

. . . .

. . . .

John Mark's mother hosted the Jerusalem church (Acts 12:12). Perhaps he had abandoned Paul and Barnabas (13:13) because he was uneasy with direct ministry to Gentiles. Maybe his report of what was happening prompted Pharisaic believers to spread out and insist on circumcision of Gentile Christians (15:1). If this were true, how would it explain Paul's objection to John Mark?

. . . .

. . . .

◆ ◆ ◆ ◆ ◆ ◆ ◆ ◆

♀ CONSIDER THIS

Read the *WILSB* feature "Barnabas—A Model for Mentoring" (Acts 9:27). "[Barnabas] stood up to Paul over a negative assessment of young John Mark (15:26–38). Notice: Encouragers like Barnabas need not avoid conflict." Barnabas seemed certain that his young nephew agreed totally with the decision of the Jerusalem council and was ready for Gentile ministry.

Circle the number on the following scale that best represents how you respond to the tension between truth and love.

1	2	3	4	5	5	4	3	2	1
TRUTH AT ALL COST		TRUTH & A TRACE OF LOVE		LOVE & TRUTH IN BALANCE		LOVE & A TRACE OF TRUTH		HARMONY AT ALL COST	

How can you improve your ability to respond to the tension between truth and love?

. . . .

. . . .

◆   ◆   ◆   ◆   ◆   ◆   ◆   ◆

CONSIDER THIS

Read the *WILSB* feature "John Mark—'Useful for Ministry'" (Acts 15:37–39). "John Mark is a case study in second chances. . . . Thanks to Barnabas, John Mark turned out to be a special gift to the early church."

Who has believed in you in the past and given you second chances when you've failed? What has that meant to your spiritual growth?

. . . .

. . . .

Who in your church or small group needs someone to help them become useful again? How can you help?

. . . .

. . . .

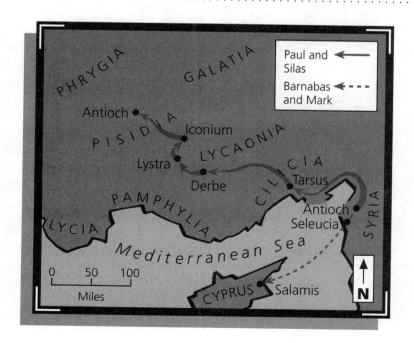

Silas is the Greek form of the Hebrew name Saul, so he and Paul shared the same Hebrew name. In Latin Silas was called Silvanus, and so his name appears in the letters Paul dictated to him (for example, 1 Thess. 1:1; 2 Thess. 1:1). Silas added his authority as a spokesman for the Jerusalem church and council to Paul's mission. What did Paul and Silas set out to do? (Acts 15:40; 16:4)

· ·

· ·

Describe the first coworker Paul selected from the newly established churches in Asia Minor. (Acts 16:1–3)

· ·

· ·

Paul and Silas probably intended to continue west on the Via Sebaste to Ephesus, the greatest city in all of Asia Minor. How did the Lord direct them otherwise? (Acts 16:6–9). (Notice the different references to deity in vv. 6, 7, 10.)

· ·

· ·

How many different ways have you experienced direction from the Lord in the last year?

. . . .

. . . .

◆ ◆ ◆ ◆ ◆ ◆ ◆ ◆

——— ◆   MANY FACES OF FREEDOM   ◆ ———
(Acts 16:11–34)

From Acts 16:10–17, Luke used the pronoun "we" to describe the activities of Paul and Silas. This is the first of four "we" passages in Acts (the others are 20:5–15, 21:1–18, and 27:1—28:16). It's likely that Luke lived at Philippi (the first "we" passage ends at Philippi and the second begins there). He gave more space to Paul's brief ministry there than the much longer ones at Corinth and Ephesus. Consequently we get unusual insights into the conversions of three Philippians.

◆ ◆ ◆ ◆ ◆ ◆ ◆ ◆

🌍 YOU ARE THERE

Read the *WILSB* features "Philippi" and "Philippi—Gateway for the Gospel" (Acts 16:12). "Just as all roads led to Rome, so much of the traffic to Rome from the east funneled through Philippi, which served as a gateway to Greece and Italy. Thus the city served as a gateway for the gospel once a church was established there."

What can you surmise from Acts 16 about the kind of place Philippi was? (vv. 12, 16, 20–23, 35–39)

. . . .

. . . .

Jewish customs required ten males as the minimum population in a town before a synagogue could be established. In the absence of a synagogue, a small Jewish community could establish a place of prayer near a source of running water needed for purification rituals. Paul and Silas found such a small group by the River Gangites about a mile and a half outside Philippi. Lydia was a God-fearing Gentile businesswoman from Thyatira in Asia Minor who frequented the place of prayer. Describe her conversion and its effects on her life. (Acts 16:14–15)

. . . .

. . . .

How have you seen people of influence who are Christians exercise their sense of responsibility to further the spread of the gospel?

. . . .

. . . .

The second Philippian convert Luke mentioned was a young slave girl. How many kinds of bondage do you think the slave girl was subject to? (Acts 16:16–19)

. . . .

. . . .

Why do you think Paul was so troubled by the ongoing publicity created by the demon-possessed girl? (Acts 16:18)

. . . .

. . . .

Assuming the slave girl believed in Jesus following her exorcism, what support might she have needed from the fledgling church developing there?

. . . .

. . . .

◆ ◆ ◆ ◆ ◆ ◆ ◆ ◆

CONSIDER THIS

Read the *WILSB* features "Be Willing to Pay the Price" (Acts 16:16–24) and "People, Property, and Profitability" (16:19). "The gospel frequently challenges systems of privilege, oppression, and injustice."

Where do you draw the lines in your work so that people and the truth aren't sacrificed to profit and expediency? Give an example.

. . . .

. . . .

Paul and Silas hurt the business of the slave girl's owners when they expelled her demon. Is there an unjust or unethical practice you should risk exposing at work, at church, or in a volunteer organization you assist? What consequences would you face?

. . . .

. . . .

The third Philippian convert Luke told about was the commander of the local jail. What events in Acts 16 could have prepared the jailer's heart so that he cried out to Paul and Silas, "Sirs, what must I do to be saved?" (v. 30)

. . . .

. . . .

Describe the conversion of the jailer and its immediate effects on his life? (Acts 16:30–34)

. . . .

. . . .

What do you think the Philippian church must have been like if Luke, Lydia, the slave girl, and the jailer were representative of its membership?

. . . .

. . . .

◆ ◆ ◆ ◆ ◆ ◆ ◆ ◆

───── ◆ DRIVEN OUT OF TOWN ◆ ─────
(Acts 16:35—17:15)

Even as there were various reasons for responding to the gospel of Jesus Christ, there were also various reasons for rejecting it. Paul and Silas were beaten, imprisoned, and asked to leave Philippi for economic reasons and, perhaps, because of anti-Semitism. Further into the provinces of Macedonia and Achaia, the reasons for rejection were quite different.

The Roman rulers of Philippi had acted impulsively and harshly in punishing Paul and Silas (Acts 16:22–24). How did they behave when they found out that Paul and Silas were Roman citizens? (vv. 35–39)

. . . .

. . . .

On what terms did Paul and Barnabas leave Philippi? (Acts 16:40)

. . . .

. . . .

Thessalonica, a city of 200,000 people, was the capital of Macedonia. A large Jewish community flourished there. Thessalonica was a more strategic center than Philippi for reaching the whole peninsula with the gospel.[3] Describe Paul and Silas's ministry in Thessalonica according to the following topics. (Acts 17:1–4)

◆ Approach

. . . .

. . . .

◆ Message

. . . .

. . . .

◆ Results

. . . .

. . . .

Describe the opposition of the unbelieving Jews to the ministry of Paul and Silas according to the following topics. (Acts 17:5–9)

◆ Approach

. . . .

. . . .

◆ Message

. . . .

. . . .

◆ Results

. . . .

. . . .

On what terms did Paul and Silas leave Thessalonica? (Acts 17:10)

. . . .

. . . .

Berea was a town off the main highway that linked Philippi and Thessalonica. Summarize what happened at Berea in each of these areas. (Acts 17:11–15)

◆ Evangelization

. . . .
. . . .

◆ Opposition

. . . .
. . . .

◆ Departure

. . . .
. . . .

How do the converts in Thessalonica and Berea (Acts 17:4, 12) compare with those from Philippi?

. . . .
. . . .

On what basis did the believers in Thessalonica and Berea trust Christ? (Acts 17:2–4, 11)

. . . .
. . . .

What was the motive for expelling the missionaries in each of these cities?

◆ Philippi

. . . .
. . . .

◆ Thessalonica

. . . .
. . . .

◆ Berea

. . . .
. . . .

What do you think are the main reasons people reject the gospel of Jesus Christ and its messengers today?

. . . .
. . . .

◆ ◆ ◆ ◆ ◆ ◆ ◆ ◆

——— ◆   FOOD FOR THOUGHT   ◆ ———
(Acts 17:17–38)

Paul arrived at Athens alone and intended to wait for Silas to come from Thessalonica before engaging in any preaching. But that's not the way things developed, and Paul eventually delivered an unusual message—one aimed at an intellectual audience who had no familiarity with the Old Testament or Jewish beliefs.

Athens had declined to a population of about 10,000, but it symbolized the glory days of Greek art and philosophy some five centuries earlier. Its citizens still prided themselves on leading the world in culture. How did Paul assess Athens? (Acts 17:16)

. . . .
. . . .

What did he do in response to his agitation about Athens? (Acts 17:17)

. . . .
. . . .

How did the Athenian philosophers react to Paul? (Acts 17:18–21)

. . . .

. . . .

◆ ◆ ◆ ◆ ◆ ◆ ◆ ◆

CONSIDER THIS

Read the *WILSB* feature "Adapt Your Witness" (Acts 17:17). "God has appointed you to your workplace to carry the message of Christ to your co-workers and customers, just as he appointed Paul to go to the agora of Athens."

What seems to be the most effective ways to influence those around your place of work?

◆ Non-verbally

. . . .

. . . .

◆ Verbally

. . . .

. . . .

Does your workplace respond to the gospel more like Thessalonica, Berea, or Athens? Why do you say so?

. . . .

. . . .

The Athenian council rejected the idea of the resurrection from the dead (Acts 17:32). However, they accepted the ideas in the first part of Paul's presentation. What had Paul said about these topics?

◆ God (Acts 17:23–25)

. . . .

. . . .

◆ Man (Acts 17:26–28)

. . . .

. . . .

◆ Response to God (Acts 17:29–31)

. . . .

. . . .

◆ ◆ ◆ ◆ ◆ ◆ ◆ ◆

CONSIDER THIS

Read the *WILSB* features "Paul, Apostle to the Intellectuals" (Acts 17:15–34) and "Dionysius and Damaris" (Acts 17:34). "Those that God calls to work within the academic disciplines have an outstanding model to follow—Paul, God's apostle to the intellectuals."

What were the results of Paul's ministry to the Areopagus, the Athenian council? (Acts 17:32–34)

. . . .
. . . .

Why do you think many intellectuals reject faith in Christ?

. . . .
. . . .

Why do you think some intellectuals respond to Christ with whole-hearted faith?

. . . .
. . . .

1. William R. Halliday, *Depths of the Earth* (New York: Harper and Row, Publishers, 1966), 113–118.
2. Richard N. Longenecker, "The Acts of the Apostles," *The Expositor's Bible Commentary,* Vol. 9 (Grand Rapids, MI: Zondervan Publishing House, 1981), 456.
3. *Ibid.,* 468.

DEEP ROOTS IN NEW SOIL

Acts 18:1—20:38

To the Greeks, mountains protected but separated people, whereas the sea, while frightening, united people."[1] The Greeks of Paul's day treated the Aegean Sea as a lake dotted with hundreds of populated islands that made travel by ship anywhere in the Aegean a series of short, safe hops.

We automatically think of Greece as Europe and Asia Minor as Asia—totally different continents, worlds apart. But in the first century the east coast cities of Greece and Macedonia and the west coast cities of Asia Minor shared the same culture. They were neighbors in a neighborhood united by the sea and its stepping-stone islands. Those same cities often felt distant from nearby inland cities over the steep mountains.

As you read Acts 18—20, you will notice that Paul and his friends were all over the Aegean basin. Names of cities and islands seem to clutter some passages. To the readers of Luke's day, all of this highlighted the bustling, energetic world in which the heyday of Paul's missionary career took place. The Aegean coastland and islands proved fertile soil for an abundant harvest of believers in Jesus Christ.

CORINTH:
◆ # TREASURE IN A CESSPOOL ◆
(Acts 18:1–17)

When Paul arrived at Corinth in the fall of A.D. 50,[2] he probably was wondering about the success of this second missionary adventure. He had been beaten and expelled at Philippi, hounded by Jewish mobs from Thessalonica and Berea, and scorned in Athens. It is likely that Paul expected Corinth to be more resistant than any of the other communities. Situated on a narrow isthmus, Corinth controlled east-west shipping between Asia Minor and Italy. It was the largest city in Greece, the wealthiest, the most cosmopolitan, and the most immoral.

What did Paul do while he continued waiting for Silas and Timothy to come from Thessalonica? (Acts 18:1–4)

. . . .

. . . .

How did he change his pattern of behavior after Silas and Timothy came? (Acts 18:5–8)

. . . .

. . . .

◆ ◆ ◆ ◆ ◆ ◆ ◆ ◆

♀ CONSIDER THIS

Read the *Word in Life Study Bible (WILSB)* feature "'Not Many Mighty' . . . But a Few" (Acts 18:7–8). "A majority of converts to early Christianity, at least those in Corinth, were from the lower classes. . . . But even if there were not many mighty, there were some."

Although Silas continued with him as his partner, Luke usually referred to Paul alone through the remainder of Acts. Silas was still important to Paul. Once his companions arrived, how did Paul show strong resolve to penetrate Corinth with the gospel? (Acts 18:5–8)

. . . .

. . . .

How did the faith of the few prominent converts influence the masses of ordinary people? (Acts 18:7–8)

. . . .

. . . .

◆ ◆ ◆ ◆ ◆ ◆ ◆ ◆

CONSIDER THIS

Read the *WILSB* feature "Afraid in the City?" (Acts 18:9–10). "Paul derived comfort from the affirmation that God was at work in the city. It was not a strange place for him, nor a place of alienation and fear. He felt at home there."

What do you think the Lord's assurance of success in Corinth meant to Paul in light of his experiences in Macedonia and Athens?

. . . .

. . . .

Paul was not spared troubles in Corinth; he was protected amid the troubles. What modern urban terrors would you ask God to protect you from if you were an urban missionary?

. . . .

. . . .

For eighteen months (Acts 18:11), Paul enjoyed an uninterrupted, successful ministry in Corinth, the most unlikely city in the Roman Empire to embrace the gospel. In July of A.D. 51, partway through Paul's stay in Corinth, Gallio was appointed proconsul for Achaia.[3] How did the unhappy Jewish authorities try to take advantage of Gallio's arrival? (Acts 18:12–13)

. . . .

. . . .

Gallio's ruling established a precedent in Roman courts by treating Christianity as a variant of Judaism, a recognized religion in the empire. How did Gallio show his disdain for the frustrated Jews? (Acts 18:16–17)

. . . .

. . . .

◆ ◆ ◆ ◆ ◆ ◆ ◆ ◆

EPHESUS:
◆ ## CENTER FOR OUTREACH ◆
(Acts 18:18—19:10)

Opposite Corinth on the east side of the Aegean Sea stood Ephesus, proud of its role as leading city of the province of Asia and guardian of the temple of Diana, one of the seven wonders of the ancient world. When Paul completed his ministry in Corinth, the Lord directed him to an even longer and more fruitful one in Ephesus. Through these two cities, the Aegean basin would become a Christian region.

How did the ministry to Ephesus begin? (Acts 18:15–22)

. . . .

. . . .

Paul's vow may have been his response to the Lord's promise of a successful ministry in Corinth (Acts 18:9–10). The hair he shaved off in Cenchrea (v. 18) had to be offered at the temple in Jerusalem (v. 22). Paul remained very much a Jewish Christian. What did Paul do between his first and second visits to Ephesus? (Acts 18:22–23)

. . . .

. . . .

Ephesus would prove to be a place of encounters with unusual religious beliefs. While Paul was absent, Apollos came to Ephesus from Alexandria in Egypt. What was unusual about his faith? (Acts 18:24–25)

. . . .

. . . .

❖ ❖ ❖ ❖ ❖ ❖ ❖ ❖

🔍 A CLOSER LOOK

Read the *WILSB* features "A Strategic Partnership" (Acts 18:2), "Marketplace Mentors: Priscilla and Aquila" (18:24–26), and "Priscilla and Aquila" (Romans 16:3–5). "Priscilla and Aquila served as spiritual mentors to Apollos (vv. 24-28), updating his theology and increasing his effectiveness in the spread of the gospel."

Priscilla and Aquila had left Rome because of Emperor Claudius's decree (A.D. 49–50) expelling all Jews from the capital. They had assisted Paul in Corinth (Acts 18:2–3). In Ephesus, they prepared the way for the apostle to return. How did Priscilla and Aquila's mentoring benefit both Ephesus and Corinth? (Acts 18:26–28)

. . . .

. . . .

When Paul reached Ephesus after visiting the interior churches founded during his first missionary journey with Barnabas, his first spiritual encounter was with an unusual group of Jews. (Acts 19:1–7)

How does this group remind you of Apollos?

. . . .

. . . .

How do they remind you of the twelve apostles on Pentecost?

. . . .

. . . .

What do you think they suggest about the readiness of the spiritual harvest in Ephesus?

. . . .

. . . .

During Paul's ministry in Ephesus, the entire province of Asia was evangelized—probably both by people coming from other cities to Ephesus and by evangelists going out from Ephesus to interior towns (Acts 19:10). Describe the two phases of Paul's Ephesian ministry.

◆ The first three months (Acts 19:8–9)

. . . .

. . . .

◆ The remaining two years (Acts 19:9–10)

. . . .

. . . .

◆ ◆ ◆ ◆ ◆ ◆ ◆ ◆

CHALLENGING
—— ◆ THE HEART OF A CITY ◆ ——
(Acts 19:11–41)

Not only did Paul's ministry in Ephesus have breadth (Acts 19:10), but it had depth. By the end of two years, the whole social fabric of Ephesus began to feel the influence of Christian values and practices. Needless to say, some people didn't like it—some because their influence was threatened, some because their immorality was exposed, and some because they were losing money.

Ephesus was noted for occultism. Not surprisingly, the Lord revealed His true powers of light in distinction to the false powers of darkness. Paul must have worked again with Priscilla and Aquila because the "handkerchiefs or aprons" (Acts 19:12) were rags for wiping away perspiration and work aprons for protecting clothing.[4] What did the incident involving the sons of Sceva establish about the power of the name of Jesus? (Acts 19:11–17)

. . . .

. . . .

How did the Ephesian believers show they truly renounced occultism for faith in Jesus? (Acts 19:18–20)

. . . .

. . . .

What occult practices does "the word of the Lord" (Acts 19:20) need to prevail over today in your world?

. . . .

. . . .

🔍 A CLOSER LOOK

Near the end of his two years in Ephesus, Paul prepared to start the final phase of his lifework. Read the *WILSB* feature "Rome or Bust" (Acts 19:21). "A tiny group living on the periphery of the Roman Empire aimed to conquer the cities and even the capital of the mightiest empire in world history with its new and strange beliefs. Incredibly, the movement prevailed!"

Because of population patterns and church growth trends, some analysts think that Asia and South America are the continents where the future of Christianity will be shaped. How can the European and North American churches help prepare the Asian and South American churches for the future?

. . . .

. . . .

What do you think are the ten key cities in the world for influencing the world for the next hundred years?

. . . .

. . . .

As more and more Ephesians put their faith in Christ as Savior, how was the local economy adversely affected? (Acts 19:23–27)

. . . .

. . . .

The open-air theater in Ephesus seated nearly 25,000.[5] What evidence did Luke provide that the Ephesian mob was dangerously out of control? (Acts 19:28–34)

. . . .

. . . .

How did Roman law as used by the city clerk once again protect the Christian church from lawless people? (Acts 19:35–41).

. . . .

. . . .

CONSIDER THIS

Read the *WILSB* feature "The Ephesus Approach: How the Gospel Penetrated a City" (Acts 19:8–41). "Evangelism in Ephesus was explosive and unpredictable. People from vastly different backgrounds formed a diverse coalition of believers who had a far-reaching impact on the city's culture and economy."

How do you think the gospel should affect these systems of a community?

◆ Health care

. . . .

. . . .

◆ Economy

. . . .

. . . .

◆ Education

. . . .

. . . .

◆ Government and Laws

. . . .

. . . .

—— ◆ Cultivating Tender Plants ◆ ——
(Acts 20:1–16)

Before heading back to Jerusalem and (hopefully) on to Rome, Paul retraced his steps around the Aegean basin to encourage the many churches that had sprung up in the preceding five years or so (Acts 20:1–3). The spiritual soil in the region was good, and Paul wanted to be sure the roots of the churches were sinking deeply into faith, hope, and love based on the truth of the gospel.

CONSIDER THIS

Read the *WILSB* feature "An International Work Group" (Acts 20:4). "The rapidly growing Christian movement recruited members from a wide variety of places." Paul's return to Jerusalem was diverted by a Jewish plot to kill him on board ship (Acts 20:3), but it was bolstered by a band of fellow-travelers from everywhere he had proclaimed the gospel. What cities or areas were represented by Paul's companions? (Notice Luke rejoins them at 20:5.) (Acts 20:4–5)

. . . .

. . . .

CONSIDER THIS

Read the *WILSB* feature "Develop Faith Whenever You Can" (Acts 20:7–12). "The incidents at Troas (vv. 7–12) reflect a habit that believers do well to cultivate—gathering frequently in informal, small clusters to reflect on Scripture, pray, and support one another." Troas was back in Asia Minor, ten miles from the site of ancient Troy.

When have you been so eager to grow spiritually that you sacrificed time and endured inconvenience to learn about the Lord?

. . . .

. . . .

How can a tragedy like Eutychus's fatal fall lead to spiritual insight and trust in the Lord?

. . . .

. . . .

Why did Paul decide to bypass Ephesus on his journey to Jerusalem? (Acts 20:13–16)

. . . .

. . . .

Why do you think Paul gave seven days to the believers in Troas and none to the Ephesians on this trip devoted to encouraging the young churches? (Acts 20:6, 16)

. . . .

. . . .

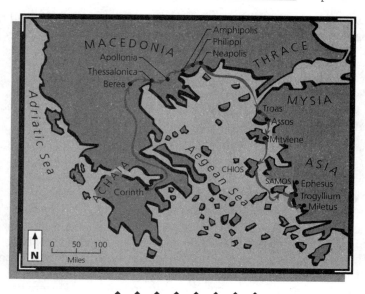

❖ ❖ ❖ ❖ ❖ ❖ ❖ ❖

In Acts Paul frequently revisited churches he established (Acts 14:21–23; 15:36, 41; 16:4–5; 18:22–23; 20:1–12). During this same period of time, he was writing the epistles of Galatians, 1 and 2 Thessalonians, 1 and 2 Corinthians, and Romans. How should we follow up on people we lead to the Lord or minister in other significant ways?

. . . .
. . . .

──── ◆ IF THIS WERE YOUR LAST GOOD-BYE ◆ ────
(Acts 20:17–38)

Paul had not trusted himself to re-enter the vast web of warm relationships he had so recently formed in Ephesus. He knew, however, that he must have a final word with the leaders entrusted with the care of this vital Asian church. These verses contain perhaps the clearest statement of Paul's attitude toward his ministry for the Lord.

What can you learn from Paul's description of his two-year ministry to the Ephesians that you want to be true of your witness for Christ? (Acts 20:18–21, 25–27)

. . . .
. . . .

107

What can you learn from Paul's description of his attitude toward his future that can help you face yours with faith and courage? (Acts 20:22–24)

. . . .

. . . .

What can you learn from Paul's warning to the Ephesian elders that can prepare you for leadership in your church? (Acts 20:28–32)

. . . .

. . . .

CONSIDER THIS

Read the *WILSB* feature "I Have Not Coveted" (Acts 20:33–38). "These words merit our attention. First, they reveal a biblical work ethic that forsakes greed in favor of hard, honest labor and a trust in God to provide for basic needs. Then, as God blesses, a worker's abundance should overflow into generosity toward others in need."

Which do you need to emphasize more to bring your life into balance: hard work or generosity? Why do you say so?

. . . .

. . . .

What do you need to do or change to correct this imbalance?

. . . .

. . . .

Who would you hate to say good-bye to for the last time as the Ephesians hated saying farewell to Paul? (Acts 20:36–38)

. . . .

. . . .

Circle the letter of the calling(s) below that you can imagine God taking you away from your family or friends to accomplish.

   a. Seminary education and the pastorate

   b. Investing retirement years in ministry abroad

   c. Full-time overseas missionary ministry

   d. Parachurch ministry with youth or college-age people

   e. Short-term missionary work related to your education and training

1. Richard N. Longenecker, "The Acts of the Apostles," _The Expositor's Bible Commentary_, Vol. 9 (Grand Rapids, MI: Zondervan Publishing House, 1981), 458.

2. _Ibid._, 485.

3. Craig S. Keener, _The IVP Bible Background Commentary: New Testament_ (Downers Grove, IL: InterVarsity Press, 1993), 376.

4. _Ibid._, 378.

5. _Ibid._, 380.

THE WITNESS REACHES METROPOLIS

Acts 21:1—28:31

Paul expected that the gospel of Jesus Christ would arrive in Rome in the same manner it had entered the major cities of the eastern Mediterranean world. Accordingly, the apostle had decided how to travel to Rome and even where he would go from there. The Lord, however, had a very different strategy for conquering the capital of the empire.

He sent His messenger to the leading city of the world as a prisoner—not as an honored orator or visiting dignitary. In one sense, the gospel arrived at Rome as humbly as the King of kings had come to the earth. In another sense, the gospel arrived as a secret conqueror. All along the journey from Caesarea to Italy, God intervened to guard the messenger and the message. Everyone on the voyage knew that Paul had been the central figure in every adventure. There could be no doubt that the prisoner was in charge.

You Can't Go Home Again

Acts 21:1—23:30

The Jerusalem Paul entered for Pentecost in A.D. 58 differed markedly from the city where Peter preached his Pentecostal message a quarter-century before. The turmoil that would climax in the destruction of Jerusalem and Jewish culture in Palestine after another decade was reaching dangerous levels. Violence, as reflected in the sanctioned plot against Paul's life (Acts 23:12–15), made Jerusalem and Judea dangerous places.

Most deadly of all were the *sicarii*, a band of terrorists whose sole purpose was to assassinate those associated with or cooperating with the Roman government of Judea. A *sicarius* was an ugly, curved dagger that was the signature weapon of these fanatics. Their favorite place of assassination was the temple complex. They felt the temple was the appropriate place to "cleanse the nation" of traitors.

The church in Jerusalem was continuing to maintain its witness in an increasingly nationalistic and violent environment. By favoring a universal gospel, Paul caused problems for the local church made up of believing Jews. He also risked his life moving around a city and countryside where assassination had become a recognized religious and political statement.

◆ ◆ ◆ ◆ ◆ ◆ ◆ ◆

◆ Dealing with Danger Signs ◆

(Acts 21:1–26)

Once again the unifying genius of the Holy Spirit emerged through the leaders of the church. The Jerusalem church leaders would not repudiate Paul's Gentile ministry in order to enhance their prestige with its separatist members. Paul agreed to practice his Judaism publicly to show the general populace that he was not an enemy of Moses or the Law. Nobody denied their convictions; nobody picked a fight to make a point.

Luke included a lot of detail about the journey from Miletus to Palestine (Acts 21:1–6), because he accompanied Paul (notice the "we" references). The looming danger for Paul in Jerusalem seems to have fixed this trip clearly in

Luke's mind. What important moment(s) in your life stand out in detail in your memory? Why?

. . . .

. . . .

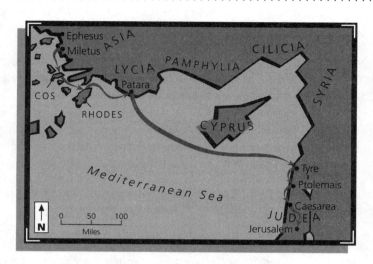

The Holy Spirit prepared many people in advance for Paul's imprisonment in Jerusalem (Acts 20:22–23; 21:4, 10–12). Paul's friends regularly interpreted the prediction as a warning that Paul should not go there (especially 21:4).

How did Paul understand the prophetic messages about danger awaiting him in Jerusalem? (20:24; 21:13–14)

. . . .

. . . .

How do you think you can tell the difference between the leading of God and the protective concern of friends?

. . . .

. . . .

◆ ◆ ◆ ◆ ◆ ◆ ◆ ◆

CONSIDER THIS

Read the *Word in Life Study Bible (WILSB)* feature "The Four Daughters of Philip" (Acts 21:9). Twenty years had passed since Philip first arrived in

Caesarea after the martyrdom of Stephen (Acts 8:40). He had raised a family of four daughters who forsook marriage for a life of prophetic ministry (21:8–9). Interview (in person or by telephone) a godly woman who has a significant ministry for the Lord in your church or on a larger scale and record her story about how God led her into that spiritual work.

. . . .

. . . .

Travel throughout Judea had become dangerous because of bands of thieves and assassins. An escort from Caesarea provided security for Paul's travel party between Caesarea and Jerusalem (Acts 21:15–16). The church even sent along Mnason, who could furnish Jerusalem lodgings for Paul. When have you received unusual hospitality from fellow Christians who were concerned about you?

. . . .

. . . .

How did the Jerusalem church leaders respond to news of Paul's ministry among the Gentiles? (Acts 21:17–19)

. . . .

. . . .

How did the Jerusalem church leaders describe the dilemma Paul's presence caused for them? (Acts 21:20–22)

. . . .

. . . .

How did the Jerusalem church leaders propose that Paul silence the false criticism that was being aimed at him? (Acts 21:23–24)

. . . .

. . . .

When the time period of a Nazirite vow expired, the one who made the vow shaved his head and brought the hair to the temple, where it was burned during a seven-day priestly ritual. A fee had to be paid for this ceremony, and many poor Jews could not afford it. It was considered an act of great piety to underwrite the expenses of impoverished Nazirites (Acts 21:26). How could Paul and the Jerusalem Christians continue to participate in Jewish culture without compromising their faith in Christ?

. . . .

. . . .

What are some contemporary cultural practices and attitudes that seem valuable to you and do not conflict with the gospel of Jesus Christ?

. . . .

. . . .

What are some contemporary cultural practices and attitudes that you avoid because you believe they conflict with the gospel of Jesus Christ?

. . . .

. . . .

◆ ◆ ◆ ◆ ◆ ◆ ◆ ◆

—— ◆ RESPONDING TO A RIOT ◆ ——
(Acts 21:27—22:22)

Paul had listened to the warnings of danger in Jerusalem, but he had not tried to escape his responsibility. Along with the Jerusalem church leaders, Paul tried to avert the hostility of the Jews who were spreading false reports of his attitudes and teaching about the Law of Moses. Sometimes our very best efforts cannot prevent trouble.

Just before the seven-day ceremonial period ended to mark the completion of the Nazirite vows, Jews from the province of Asia (where Ephesus was) saw Paul in the temple and started a riot. What was their charge against him and its basis? (Acts 21:27–29)

. . . .

. . . .

Compare and contrast the behaviors of Jerusalem (represented by the temple mob) and Rome (represented by the Roman commander) toward Paul. (Acts 21:30–39)

JERUSALEM   ROME

. . . .

. . . .

Describe a situation in which unbelievers were more understanding of you than religious people. How did that situation make you feel?

. . . .

. . . .

◆ ◆ ◆ ◆ ◆ ◆ ◆ ◆

CONSIDER THIS

Read the *WILSB* feature "The Jerusalem Riots" (Acts 21:30). "To preach in a city is one thing; to occupy and transform it is quite another." Why do you think the Jerusalem church could not transform the city so that it would accept spiritual ministry to Gentiles?

. . . .

. . . .

Why do you think churches today tend to desert cities for the suburbs?

. . . .

. . . .

What ministry challenges do you think churches that choose to stay in the cities should accept in order to "occupy and transform" their communities?

. . . .

. . . .

What opportunities are gained when a person knows how to "speak the language" of those he or she wants to influence? (Acts 21:37–40)

. . . .

. . . .

What common ground could Paul claim to share with his attackers? (Acts 21:2–5)

. . . .

. . . .

What things about Paul's conversion account would appeal to his Jewish audience? (Acts 21:6–11)

. . . .

. . . .

What features of Paul's call to serve God probably sounded good to the Jewish crowd? (Acts 21:12–20)

. . . .

. . . .

With all that they could agree with Paul about, why do you think the one point of disagreement outweighed everything else? (Acts 21:21–22)

. . . .

. . . .

Traditional Judaism had defined itself in exclusive terms. Jews were better than all non-Jews. What traditional practices or beliefs are Christians you know tempted to use as evidence they are better than unbelievers (and, perhaps, other Christians)?

. . . .

. . . .

◆ ◆ ◆ ◆ ◆ ◆ ◆ ◆

──── ◆ MANAGING TO MANAGE ◆ ────
THE MANAGERS
(Acts 22:23—23:9)

Paul had been assaulted by the Jerusalem mob and then arrested by the Roman army. We have no idea how badly injured he was before the soldiers rescued Paul or how roughly the troops treated him as they took him into custody. But we see right away that Paul took command of the situation rather than reacting in terror or self-pity. He accepted this life-threatening situation as the will of God (Acts 20:24; 21:13–14) and responded with personal courage and faith in God.

In their initial rage, the temple mob had physically attacked Paul (Acts 21:30-31). They were reduced by the presence of Roman soldiers to throwing dirt and ripping their own clothes (22:23). While the Jews appeared increasingly hostile but impotent, Paul appeared increasingly in control. How did he manage the Roman commander? (Acts 22:23–29)

. . . .

. . . .

◆ ◆ ◆ ◆ ◆ ◆ ◆ ◆

CONSIDER THIS
Read the *WILSB* feature "Faith and Rights" (Acts 22:25–29). "There's no need to allow discrimination to hinder one's practice of Christianity in society, particularly in one's workplace."

How have you seen pressure put on Christians to refrain from expressing their faith in public settings?

. . . .

. . . .

How can Christians today, like Paul back then, assert their rights without being overbearing or pushy?

. . . .

. . . .

❖ ❖ ❖ ❖ ❖ ❖ ❖ ❖

CONSIDER THIS

Read the *WILSB* feature "Paul Apologized for Losing His Cool" (Acts 23:5). "Would you be willing to apologize for losing your cool, even if your opponent were attacking you and your values?"

How did Paul show maturity and self-control by the way he recovered from his loss of temper at the high priest Ananias? (Acts 22:30—23:5)

. . . .

. . . .

How did Paul manage the Jewish council which was determined to condemn him to death? (Acts 23:6–10)

. . . .

. . . .

How do you want to react when important people around you criticize you?

. . . .

. . . .

What can you learn from the way Paul reacted to the Roman commander and the Jewish leaders that would help you react with courage and faith rather than fear or anger?

. . . .

. . . .

❖ ❖ ❖ ❖ ❖ ❖ ❖ ❖

◆ FREED FROM FANATICAL FOES ◆
(Acts 23:10–30)

So far the story of Paul's encounter with the Jerusalem mob has revealed the benefits of Roman law and the courage of Paul in the face of danger. Neither of those was adequate to extricate Paul from the danger he faced in Jerusalem. But Paul had come there in full assurance that he was fulfilling a mission God had given him. In the final analysis, Paul's confidence was in the Lord.

How did each of the following react to the raucous stalemate within the Sanhedrin over Paul's guilt or innocence?

◆ The Romans (Acts 23:10)

. . . .

◆ God (Acts 23:11)

. . . .

◆ The Jews (Acts 23:12–15)

. . . .

"The commander's assignment of two hundred soldiers with the centurions . . . to guard Paul would weaken the garrison in Jerusalem's fortress Antonia by as much as one-third; thus they must return quickly (23:32). The two hundred spearmen are non-Roman light auxiliary infantry. If the Antonia cohort included a regular cavalry unit, it had as many as one hundred horsemen—hence the commander sends most of them with Paul. Given the unrest in Palestine and night attack by robbers, a smaller contingent would not be safe in the hills of Judea at night."[1]

If you can, give a contemporary example of God using secular powers to protect and advance the spread of the gospel.

. . . .

. . . .

Felix had been born a slave in the imperial household in Rome but had been freed by the mother of Claudius, who later became emperor. Because Felix had been a childhood friend of Claudius, he advanced in government until he became governor of Judea. Felix was a brutal, unpopular ruler, whose greatest success was marrying three princesses in succession who provided him wealth and social status.[2]

What favorable impressions should Felix have received from the letter Claudius Lysias wrote the governor about Paul? (Acts 23:26–30).

. . . .

. . . .

Paul was far from free when he was surrounded by Roman soldiers and horsemen, but he was protected from the fanatical assassins in Jerusalem. How would a pessimist have evaluated Paul's situation as the apostle was transferred from Jerusalem to Caesarea?

. . . .

. . . .

What are some of the important lessons of life that God has taught you through hardships that you probably couldn't have learned any other way?

. . . .

. . . .

1. Craig S. Keener, *The IVP Bible Background Commentary: New Testament* (Downers Grove, IL: InterVarsity Press, 1993), 393.

2. Richard N. Longenecker, "The Acts of the Apostles," *The Expositor's Bible Commentary,* Vol. 9 (Grand Rapids, MI: Zondervan Publishing House, 1981), 539.

GOD IN THE DOCK

Acts 23:31—26:32

I n 1948 C. S. Lewis wrote an article for the journal Lumen Vitae *entitled* "Difficulties in Presenting the Christian Faith to Modern Unbelievers." *In it he reflected on the lessons he had learned in expressing Christianity to RAF fliers and crewmen during World War II. Since then this brief essay has been retitled "God in the Dock" and has given its name to a collection of short pieces by Lewis.*

"In the dock" is British slang for "on trial." Lewis stated, "The ancient man approached God (or even the gods) as the accused person approaches his judge. For the modern man the roles are reversed. He is the judge: God is in the dock. . . . The trial may even end in God's acquittal. But the important thing is that Man is on the Bench and God is in the Dock."[1]

The apostle Paul found himself imprisoned and on trial because Jewish authorities in Jerusalem wished to kill him. Three Roman officials in Palestine then found themselves in the uncomfortable position (for people of the ancient world) of trying to decide theological issues. Unlike modern people, they didn't want God or His spokesman in their dock, but they tried gamely to apply Roman law to the situation.

❖ ❖ ❖ ❖ ❖ ❖ ❖ ❖

───── ◆ A GREEDY, INDECISIVE JUDGE ◆ ─────
(Acts 23:31—24:26)

The Roman historian Tacitus said that Felix, "indulging in every kind of barbarity and lust, exercised the power of a king in the spirit of a slave."[2] The Jewish authorities had good reason to think that Felix would surrender Paul to be executed to keep the peace. Paul's hope was that Felix's ten years in Palestine had taught him to be suspicious of the powers in Jerusalem.

Cilicia and Judea were both part of the province of Syria during the time of Paul's imprisonment, so Felix agreed to hear the case once the soldiers delivered Paul to his palace in Caesarea (Acts 23:31–35). What strategy did the Jerusalem authorities use to sway Felix in their favor? (Acts 24:1–4, 7)

. . . .
. . . .

What charges did the Jewish authorities level against Paul? (Acts 24:5–6)

. . . .

. . . .

How did Paul respond to the charges of the temple authorities? (Acts 24:11–13, 18–19)

. . . .

. . . .

How did Paul defend his fidelity to his Jewish heritage? (Acts 24:14–17, 20–21)

. . . .

. . . .

◆ ◆ ◆ ◆ ◆ ◆ ◆ ◆

CONSIDER THIS

Read the *Word in Life Study Bible (WILSB)* feature "Truth Can Trigger Opposition" (Acts 24:1-26). "God's grace often exposes the sin and guilt of people, sometimes triggering hostility. Believers can become a convenient target of anger."

When some unbelievers are bothered by the gospel, how do they criticize the witness and the church to avoid facing their need of faith in Christ?

. . . .

. . . .

What personal needs do you think underlie these instinctive attacks by some unbelievers and how can you keep from feeling personally attacked while witnessing to the gospel?

. . . .

. . . .

What flaws in Felix's character were exposed by his ongoing contact with Paul and the gospel of Christ? (Acts 24:24–26).

. . . .

. . . .

◆ ◆ ◆ ◆ ◆ ◆ ◆ ◆

CONSIDER THIS

Read the *WILSB* feature "Paul and the Structures of Power" (Acts 24:25–26). "Chapters 23—25 make it plain that Paul was competent in and comfortable with the Roman judicial system and its procedures."

What do you think are the benefits and limitations of utilizing available political and legal processes for advancing the gospel of Christ?

Benefits . . . .

Limitations . . . .

◆ AN AGREEABLE, INEXPERIENCED JUDGE ◆
(Acts 24:27—25:12)

Nothing is known of Porcius Festus before he became governor of Judea in A.D. 59, and he died in office two years later. But the report of Josephus is that Festus was the most just and the only popular Roman governor Judea ever had. When he took office, the Jerusalem authorities wasted no time trying to settle their two-year-old score with Paul.

The Jerusalem authorities realized that Felix had kept Paul in prison as a favor to them (Acts 24:27). They feared that Festus would release Paul as soon as he reviewed his case and found no legal reason to detain him. There is no record of what Paul did during these two years, but it's unlikely that he sat around and moped.

Who has been an inspiration to you by the way they have handled enforced inactivity in a spiritually productive way? How were you inspired?

. . . .

. . . .

How did the Jewish leaders plan to deal with Paul? (Acts 25:1–3)

. . . .

. . . .

How did Festus inadvertently frustrate that plan? (Acts 25:4–55)

. . . .

. . . .

The retrial of Paul reads like a tired rehashing of old charges and defenses. What impression do you think this would have made on newly arrived Festus? (Acts 25:6–8)

. . . .

. . . .

Based on Paul's defense (Acts 25:8), what were the three charges brought against him?

. . . .

. . . .

Every Roman citizen had a right to appeal an extraordinary case to the imperial court in Rome. Since he was charged with offending Caesar (Acts 25:8), Paul's case was serious. How did Paul explain his appeal for a trial before the emperor Nero in Rome? (Acts 25:10–11)

. . . .

. . . .

CONSIDER THIS

Read the _WILSB_ feature "Caught Between a Novice and the Establishment" (Acts 25:2). "In light of Paul's example here, it's worth asking: Do you know the proper routes of appeal in your workplace or community." (You may want to discuss the following questions with a knowledgeable pastor or friend before writing out your answers.)

If your local school banned all religious expression, what route of appeal do you think you should follow?

. . . .

. . . .

If local government banned church construction in residential neighborhoods, what route of appeal do you think you should follow?

. . . .

. . . .

◆ ◆ ◆ ◆ ◆ ◆ ◆ ◆

◆ AN EXPERT, INTERESTED JUDGE ◆
(Acts 25:13—26:32)

Herod Agrippa II was the son of the Herod who died in Acts 12:23. Agrippa II governed territory adjacent to Judea, but he was appointed by Rome to supervise the priesthood and temple in Jerusalem. As far as Rome was concerned, Agrippa was the empire's resident expert on Judaism.[3]

◆ ◆ ◆ ◆ ◆ ◆ ◆ ◆

✓ FOR YOUR INFO

Read the *WILSB* feature "A Timely Diplomatic Visit" (Acts 25:13–22). "Festus, the Jews, and Paul all benefited from the couple's expertise in Jewish history and affairs."

What did Festus confess to finding surprising about the Jewish case against Paul? (Acts 25:18–19)

. . . .

. . . .

After Agrippa expressed interest in hearing Paul's defense (Acts 25:22), what kind of audience did Festus arrange for his honored guest? (v. 23)

. . . .

. . . .

What kind of assistance did Festus want from Agrippa, the expert about Jewish affairs? (Acts 25:27)

. . . .

. . . .

Luke recorded Paul's address to Agrippa and the assembled dignitaries in greater detail than his other defenses, so its contents must be important. Like Paul's other speeches, this one reflects a standard rhetorical pattern.[4] Summarize each portion of the speech.

Exordium or address to the judge (Acts 26:2–3) . . . .

Narratio or sequence of events (Acts 26:4–18)

◆ Credentials (vv. 4–8) . . . .

◆ Persecution (vv. 9–11) . . . .

◆ Conversion (vv. 12–18) . . . .

Argumentio or conclusions reached (Acts 26:19–23) . . . .

As with many pagan listeners, Festus could not comprehend talk of the resurrection of Jesus and interrupted Paul (Acts 26:24). Paul refused to be distracted and kept his focus on Agrippa. How can you tell that Paul's goal was to persuade Agrippa to believe the gospel of Jesus Christ? (vv. 25–29)

. . . .

. . . .

◆ ◆ ◆ ◆ ◆ ◆ ◆ ◆

CONSIDER THIS

Read the *WILSB* feature "Audience-Shaped Messages" (Acts 26:1–32). "The gospel itself is forever the same, but as Christ's followers we are called to shape our message to fit our various audiences."

In his essay "God in the Dock," C. S. Lewis identified three difficulties in explaining Christianity to everyday people in the modern world.[5] How have you encountered each of these in your experience?

1. People mix Christian ideas with occult and eastern concepts.

. . . .

. . . .

2. People are generally unaware and skeptical of history (the Bible), but they trust experts and scientists.

. . . .

. . . .

3. You have to translate theological terms into everyday language.

. . . .

. . . .

Circle the letter(s) of the kinds of people you regularly work or talk with.

a. People who grew up in Christian churches

b. College-educated professionals

c. Rural people with a strong work ethic

d. Blue-collar workers

e. People with new age or Eastern religious views

f. Multi-ethnic, multi-cultural mix

g. Suburbanites

h. Racially intolerant people

i. Leaders of the community

j. Athletes

k. Artistic types

l. Political conservatives

m. Political liberals

Choose three of the groups you identified in the preceding item and identify traits of each that you would want to keep in mind when sharing the gospel with someone from that group.

1 . . . .

2 . . . .

3 . . . .

Identify an individual from one of your three groups with whom you would like to share the gospel of Christ. On a separate sheet, write a synopsis of what you would say to this person, shaping the message in keeping with the group traits listed above.

1. C. S. Lewis, "God in the Dock," *God in the Dock,* ed. by Walter Hooper (Grand Rapids, MI: William B. Eerdmans Publishing Company, 1970), 244.

2. P. Cornelius Tacitus, *The Histories,* v. 9.

3. Richard N. Longenecker, "The Acts of the Apostles," *The Expositor's Bible Commentary,* Vol. 9 (Grand Rapids, MI: Zondervan Publishing House, 1981), 548.

4. Craig S. Keener, *The IVP Bible Background Commentary: New Testament* (Downers Grove IL: InterVarsity Press, 1993), 398.

5. *God in the Dock,* 240–244.

JOURNEY TO THE CENTER OF THE EARTH

Acts 27:1—28:31

In 1864 a struggling French writer published his second novel. The first one had brought him a taste of financial success after fifteen years of discouragement and rejection. Soon the writer was creating at the pace that would let him average two novels a year for the next forty years.

In the nineteenth century, there was a good deal of speculation in scientific circles about the interior of the earth. Savants proposed that the earth was hollow with openings at the poles. Lights from the interior supposedly created the auroras of the arctic and antarctic regions. Others hypothesized that volcanos might be linked by a subterranean network of passages that could offer entrance into the heart of the earth.

So Jules Verne, a failure at plays, operas, and theatrical farces, cranked that second fantastic novel from his unusual mind. In *Journey to the Centre of the Earth*, a Danish student named Axel followed the directions on an ancient Icelandic chronicle deciphered by his eccentric uncle down a volcano to the geographic center of the earth. There the explorers discovered the secrets of the prehistoric past.

When the apostle Paul journeyed to Rome as a prisoner of the emperor, he moved to the political center of the world of his day. There was nothing imaginary about this journey. And when he arrived, Paul was looking into the future. The secret of the future of Rome was the gospel of Jesus Christ.

◆ ◆ ◆ ◆ ◆ ◆ ◆

——— ◆ FROM CAPTIVE TO CAPTAIN ◆ ———
(Acts 27:1–26)

 The apostle Paul was a natural leader whose force of character soon influenced every situation. However, when he started to Rome as a prisoner, he had no standing in the eyes of the Roman escort. Because of the dangers that developed and the insights God gave Paul, he eventually became the spokesperson everyone listened to, even though he was in chains.

At the beginning of the voyage to Rome, who was firmly in charge of affairs of the journey? (Acts 27:1)

· ·

· ·

More than one Roman regiment bore the title Augustan, but it was a privilege to bear the former emperor's name.[1] Nothing can be inferred about this one or its commander other than that it served Nero directly. The other prisoners (Acts 27:1) may have appealed cases to the emperor or they may have been convicts sent to Rome to die in gladiatorial spectacles.[2] Adramyttium, the home port of the ship the centurion commandeered, was near Troas on the west coast of Asia Minor.

What was the first indication that Paul enjoyed privileges with the centurion that the other prisoners probably didn't? (Acts 27:3)

· ·

· ·

Travel from east to west in the Mediterranean Sea was always difficult because the prevailing winds blew from the west. From October to March, sailing stopped because the winds were too severe. The Alexandrian ship commandeered in Myra (Acts 27:5–6) was of the largest class sailing the sea. Egypt supplied grain to Rome and a fleet of large cargo vessels operated from Alexandria.

This second ship Paul traveled in was probably three times the size of the first one. It would have been about 180 feet long, 45 feet wide, and 40 feet deep at the keel.[3] Look ahead and note how many crew, prisoners, and escorts were on this Alexandrian grain ship. (Acts 27:37)

· ·

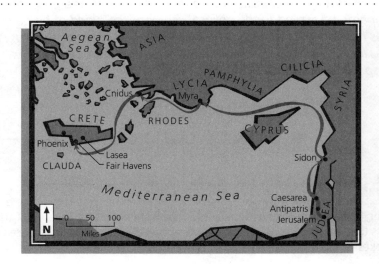

Northwesterly winds blew the Alexandrian ship away from the mainland, so it slipped into the lee of Crete (Acts 27:7). It was already after the time of the fast associated with the Day of Atonement (_Yom Kippur_) in late September or early October (v. 9). How can you tell that Paul's authority as a spokesman for God was not yet recognized? (Acts 27:9–12)

. . . .

♦ ♦ ♦ ♦ ♦ ♦ ♦ ♦

♀ CONSIDER THIS

Read the _Word in Life Study Bible (WILSB)_ feature "It Serves Them Right!" (Acts 27:9–11). "Paul's willingness to speak up (v. 10) is remarkable in that he was on his way to prison and had no need to warn anybody of anything."

Circle the letter of the statement that comes closest to matching the way you respond to the needs of people who mistreat you.

a. I hope they need my help so I can rub their noses in it.

b. I hope they find out how it feels to be mistreated.

c. They're on their own.

d. I'll help, but I won't like it.

e. I'll help because they need help.

Describe a time when the kindness you showed someone who was unfriendly later led to chances to share the gospel or form a friendship with that person.

. . . .

. . . .

When Paul's ship tried to reach a better winter harbor, it was caught in a gale that drove the ship uncontrollably for days (Acts 27:13–20). Describe the scene when Paul became the _de facto_ leader on the gale-tossed Alexandrian ship. (Acts 27:21–26)

. . . .

. . . .

Why was it important for Paul to credit God with the information he shared with the ship's crew and the Roman troops? (Acts 27:23–25)

. . . .

. . . .

In what kind of situations do you think you need to tell others that God has guided you?

. . . .

. . . .

◆ ◆ ◆ ◆ ◆ ◆ ◆ ◆

───── ◆ ORGANIZING A SHIPWRECK ◆ ─────
(Acts 27:27–44)

Even though a ship's crew may have little control over the events that cause a shipwreck, you expect the ship's leaders to react to the emergency with instructions that will minimize loss and promote safety. The surprising feature of the shipwreck at the end of Acts 27 is that Paul, the landlubber, directs the evacuation drill rather than the ship's captain. The captain seems to have had a more sinister scheme.

How did the seamen on the ship deal with the impending wreck of their vessel? (Acts 27:27–30)

. . . .

. . . .

How can you tell that Paul's authority was now completely accepted by everyone on the doomed ship? (Acts 27:31–36)

. . . .

. . . .

What promises of God do you need to remind yourself of when you face emergency situations in order to face them with greater faith and courage?

. . . .

. . . .

In the morning light, the crew picked out a beach on the coast where they hoped to land the ship (Acts 27:39). But they ran aground some distance from shore, and heavy seas started to break up the exposed stern of the ship (v. 41). How did the respect Paul had earned as a leader save his life and the lives of all the other prisoners?

. . . .

. . . .

What qualities should make Christians valuable to unbelievers who have to depend on them?

. . . .

. . . .

What qualities make some Christians annoying to unbelievers who have to depend on them?

. . . .

. . . .

List your strengths and weaknesses that would make you either valuable or annoying to an unbeliever who might have to count on you.

◆ Strengths

. . . .

. . . .

◆ Weaknesses

. . . .

. . . .

◆ ◆ ◆ ◆ ◆ ◆ ◆ ◆

◆ A HERO ENTERS ROME ◆
(Acts 28:1–16)

Through the winter months spent on Malta, Paul's prestige with his Roman escort continued to increase. By the time they continued to Italy in the spring, the apostle was honored and treated with deference. He was a prisoner, but also a celebrity.

In the course of fourteen days the gale had blown Paul's ship some 600 miles from Crete to Malta, the largest of five small islands about 60 miles south of Sicily. The Maltese natives were descendants from the same Phoenician merchants who had settled Carthage in North Africa. They spoke a Punic dialect that would hinder verbal communication with the stranded travelers.

How did Paul establish a reputation with the ordinary people of the island? (Acts 28:1–6)

. . . .

. . . .

How did the apostle establish a reputation with the Roman governor of Malta? (Acts 28:7–8)

. . . .

. . . .

What was the nature and outcome of Paul's ministry during the winter he spent in Malta? (Acts 28:9–10)

. . . .

. . . .

Paul endured fourteen days in a ship tossed by huge waves and blown by fierce winds (Acts 27:27). He swam or rode wreckage through pounding surf and driving rain from the wreck to the beach (vv. 43–44). When he finally reached land, a poisonous snake bit him (28:3). Why do you think God chose to protect Paul *through* all these dangers rather than protecting him *from* them as He took him to Rome, the center of the earth?

. . . .

. . . .

What do you think it means in your life when God delivers you *through* rather than *from* difficulties?

. . . .

. . . .

When winter was over, Paul's journey to Rome ended pleasantly. Julius the centurion commandeered another Alexandrian grain ship, this one bearing the figurehead of Castor and Pollux (Acts 28:11). They made the 60 miles to Syracuse on Sicily in a day (v. 12), a comparable distance to Rhegium on the Italian peninsula in another day (v. 13), and the full 180 miles to Puteoli in two more.

What spiritual encouragement did Paul receive to go along with pleasant sailing? (Acts 28:13–15).

. . . .

. . . .

◆ ◆ ◆ ◆ ◆ ◆ ◆ ◆

CONSIDER THIS

Read the *WILSB* feature "Joy on the Way to Jail" (Acts 28:14–15). "As Paul neared the end of his journey to face trial, believers from Rome and its environs welcomed him along the Appian Highway from Puteoli to Rome."

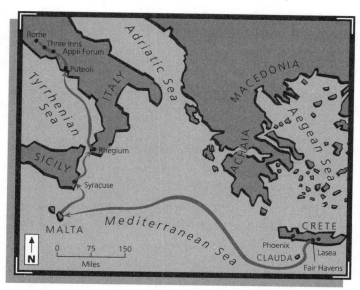

What prison ministries operate in your area? (Ask your pastor or Bible study leader if you aren't familiar with any.)

. . . .

. . . .

How do you think the gospel of Christ could provide hope to someone facing a lengthy incarceration?

. . . .

. . . .

What special arrangements were made for Paul's confinement in Rome? (Acts 28:16)

. . . .

. . . .

For several years the course of Paul's life had been moving toward Rome. He wanted to go there, and he knew God wanted him to go there. He would have sensed the direction and protection of God, but he would not have felt impervious to the dangers around him. Toward what goal do you sense that God has been directing and protecting you?

. . . .

. . . .

How do you think Paul would encourage you to strengthen your faith and courage?

. . . .

. . . .

◆ ◆ ◆ ◆ ◆ ◆ ◆ ◆

—— ◆ THE GOSPEL ENTERS ROME ◆ ——
(Acts 28:17–31)

Paul preached the gospel in Rome the same way he had proclaimed it everywhere else—to the Jews first and then to the Gentiles. As everywhere else, some believed and some didn't. Unlike everywhere else, no one in Rome tried to hinder Paul's ministry, even though he was a prisoner.

Why do you imagine Paul took the initiative to call the Jewish leaders in Rome together right away? (Acts 28:17)

. . . .

. . . .

How did Paul try to do each of the following in his initial contact with the Jews of Rome? (Acts 28:17–20).

Identify with Judaism . . . .

Assert his innocence . . . .

Create interest in the gospel . . . .

There was no united Jewish community in Rome. Every synagogue was independent of the others.[4] Apparently the Sanhedrin in Jerusalem had not forwarded charges against Paul to any of the synagogues. This may have been because Jews in Rome were keeping a low profile since being allowed to return to Rome following their expulsion by Claudius (see Acts 18:2). How did the Jews express both their courtesy and skepticism to Paul? (Acts 28:21–22)

. . . .

. . . .

What methods did Paul use to evangelize the many Jews of Rome who came to his lodging on the appointed day? (Acts 28:23)

. . . .

. . . .

How did Paul explain to the Jews of Rome his mission to the Gentiles? (Acts 28:24–28)

. . . .

. . . .

◆ ◆ ◆ ◆ ◆ ◆ ◆ ◆

CONSIDER THIS

Read the _WILSB_ feature "A Response to Rejection" (Acts 28:17–19). "As believers called to proclaim the message of Christ, our role is not to change people; that's a job for the Holy Spirit (John 16:8). Instead, we need to give a full and careful disclosure of what God has done for us, realizing that it might result in rejection."

Circle the letter of the statement that best expresses your response to anticipated rejection.

a. I can't witness for Christ if it means someone might reject me.

b. I'll speak for Christ when someone else raises the topic and minimizes the chance of rejection.

c. I witness for Christ in organized outreach efforts so that any rejection is aimed more at my church or sponsoring group.

d. I witness for Christ as graciously as I can and endure occasional rejection as an unpleasant but unavoidable consequence.

e. I witness for Christ whenever I can, and I don't care if some people resent me. That's their problem.

Which response do you want to be yours, and what can you do to become a person who will respond that way?

. . . .

. . . .

◆ ◆ ◆ ◆ ◆ ◆ ◆ ◆

⚲ CONSIDER THIS

Read the *WILSB* features "All Roads Lead to Rome—And Beyond" (Acts 28:28–31) and "Paul's Rented House" (Acts 28:30–31). "Confined to his lodgings and handcuffed to one of the soldiers who guarded him in four-hour shifts, [Paul] was free to receive visitors and talk with them about the gospel."

Why do you think Luke left the ending to Acts open rather than telling his readers exactly what happened after the gospel reached Rome?

. . . .

. . . .

In the history of your church, when did the power of the gospel of Christ make its greatest impact on your community? (If you aren't familiar with your church history, ask your pastor or an older member.)

. . . .

. . . .

How is your church currently involved in spreading the gospel of Christ to your "Jerusalem and all Judea and Samaria" right around you? (Acts 1:8)

. . . .

. . . .

How is your church currently involved in continuing the spread of the gospel to the end of the earth? (Acts 1:8)

. . . .

. . . .

1. Richard N. Longenecker, "The Acts of the Apostles," *The Expositor's Bible Commentary,* Vol. 9 (Grand Rapids, MI: Zondervan Publishing House, 1981), 558.

2. Craig S. Keener, *The IVP Bible Background Commentary: New Testament* (Downers Grove, IL: InterVarsity Press, 1993), 400.

3. *Ibid.,* 401.

4. *Ibid.,* 405–406.

LEADER'S GUIDE

Small group studies succeed when all of the group members participate in discussion. As the leader you must be well-prepared, but your task is to stimulate the other group members to discover and apply the truths of the Bible passage under discussion. Discussion questions are your primary tool for guiding Bible exploration.

Good discussion questions are open-ended. Rather than asking for short, factual answers, they invite thinking about the text; looking beyond facts for spiritual principles, they explore the implication of the biblical truth for daily life. On the other hand, questions that can be answered "yes" or "no" effectively stifle discussion.

Discussion questions fall into three general categories.

Content questions invite exploration of the biblical text. Many of the questions in the *Bible Discovery Guide* are content questions. You may use some of the *Bible Discovery Guide* questions in your group discussions, but you will want to use other content questions to summarize what they learned in the *Bible Discovery Guide*.

Implication questions stimulate discussion of possible ways a biblical passage might be applied to life.

Application questions ask group members to formulate specific plans of action that implement biblical concepts in their lives.

Most discussion questions are content questions. Fewer are implication questions. Fewer still are application questions, but these may require the most time to answer satisfactorily.

The Leader's Guide provides additional content questions to summarize biblical material. Implication and application questions are provided for use or as models for your own questions. Each session plan contains many more questions than you can use in a typical hour-long Bible study. Be selective and creative.

Manage your session time carefully. Don't spend too much time on content questions so that your group fails to get to the implication and application phases. Don't allow a talkative group member to dominate discussion. When he or she takes a breath, thank him or her and ask for comments from others. Be careful not to be the dominant talker yourself.

If your group will be filling out the *Bible Discovery Guide* as part of your session, you must decide how much time you can devote to that activity. No one can complete a lesson in twenty minutes, so you may want to assign different parts of the study to different group members, and then each can make a contribution from his or her *Bible Discovery Guide* portions. In that way, each group member will bring a piece of the puzzle to the discussion and together the group assembles the whole picture.

LESSON 1
"POWER TO THE PEOPLE!"
Acts 1:1–11

SESSION AIMS

◆ To explore the relationship of Acts to Luke
◆ To overview the structure and scope of Acts
◆ To explore the promises made in Acts to believers today regarding the power of the gospel

Read through the questions in this *Bible Discovery Guide* and select those that you want your group to discuss. Supplement those questions with any of the ones provided below. Arrange the questions in the order that seems best for your group. Be sure to familiarize yourself with the feature articles in this portion of the *Word in Life Study Bible*. These helps can greatly enrich your group's insights into God's Word.

WARMING UP

1. What is the most awesome display of power you have ever seen? How did it make you feel?
2. What is the best (or worst) sequel to a book (or movie) you ever read (saw)? What made it so good (bad)?

DIGGING IN

1. How would you summarize the evidence that Luke wrote Acts as a sequel to his Gospel?
2. How did Luke tie together the ending of his Gospel and the beginning of Acts?
3. What did you learn from this study about the kingdom of God?
4. What are the three phases of gospel expansion outlined in Acts 1:8?
5. Who are the primary characters Luke associated with each phase of gospel expansion in Acts?
6. At the time of His ascension, why did Jesus want the apostles to focus on the immediate future rather than the distant future?
7. What was the importance of the Holy Spirit for the future ministry of the apostles?
8. Do you think it was important for the apostles to witness the ascension of Jesus? Why or why not?

LOOKING FURTHER

1. How do you think the kingdom of God should express itself in your life?
2. How do you think the kingdom of God should express itself in your church?
3. What is the power like that the Holy Spirit brings into the life of an individual Christian and into the life of a group of believers?
4. Why do you think the presence and power of the Holy Spirit leads automatically to witness about Jesus?
5. What impact should the account of the ascension of Jesus have on us?

MAKING PLANS

1. What could you do to make yourself more available to the powerful Holy Spirit as a witness for Jesus?
2. What part have you played in sharing the gospel locally, nationwide, and around the world?
3. At the end of Lesson One in your _Bible Discovery Guide_ write in the margin a witnessing goal—the name of a person you want to share Christ with, an outreach program you can get involved with, a short-term missions trip you want to go on, etc. At the end of this Bible study, you will evaluate your progress toward this goal.

LESSON 2
THE WORLD AT YOUR DOORSTEP
Acts 1:12—2:47

SESSION AIMS

◆ To discover how the Spirit worked through the apostles at Pentecost and initiated a new society, the church
◆ To identify characteristics of Spirit-filled witnesses
◆ To identify and assess ways of strengthening our church communities

Read through the questions in this _Bible Discovery Guide_ and select those that you want your group to discuss. Supplement those questions with any of the ones provided below. Arrange the questions in the order that seems best for your group. Be sure to familiarize yourself with the feature articles in this portion of the _Word in Life Study Bible_. These helps can greatly enrich your group's insights into God's Word.

WARMING UP

1. Describe the setting in which you saw the most people from different nations gathered together.
2. What was the most impressive speech you ever heard? What was the outcome of it?

DIGGING IN

1. Why did the apostles feel they should replace Judas Iscariot as a witness to Jesus?
2. What were the qualifications to be an apostle? Why were these factors important?
3. How did the Holy Spirit manifest Himself when He came upon the believers gathered in Jerusalem?
4. How did the people in Jerusalem react to the arrival of the Holy Spirit?
5. Describe the crowd that gathered in response to the commotion created by the Holy Spirit.
6. What explanation did Peter give the crowd from Scripture of what was happening that day?
7. What did Peter witness about Jesus to the crowd gathered at Pentecost?
8. What course of action did Peter recommend to his listeners?
9. What behaviors characterized the followers of Jesus in Jerusalem after the arrival of the Holy Spirit?
10. How did the residents of Jerusalem initially react to the new community of believers in Jesus?

LOOKING FURTHER

1. What qualifications do you need to be a witness for Jesus? What implications does this have for the content of your witness?
2. What indicators show people today that the Holy Spirit has entered the life of a believer in Jesus?
3. How do skeptics explain away the presence of the Holy Spirit in our lives?
4. How would you like to see your church become more like the early believers at the end of Acts 2?

MAKING PLANS

1. How can you help your church be an even warmer place of openness and fellowship?

2. How can you encourage greater generosity with material possessions in your church?
3. How can you help create even more emphasis in your church on serious Bible study?

LESSON 3
GROWING PAINS
Acts 3:1—5:42

SESSION AIMS

◆ To trace the emergence of opposition to the gospel of Jesus
◆ To evaluate the courage of the apostles in the face of growing opposition
◆ To examine our courage to defend the faith and suffer for it

Read through the questions in this _Bible Discovery Guide_ and select those that you want your group to discuss. Supplement those questions with any of the ones provided below. Arrange the questions in the order that seems best for your group. Be sure to familiarize yourself with the feature articles in this portion of the _Word in Life Study Bible_. These helps can greatly enrich your group's insights into God's Word.

WARMING UP

1. When you were a child, when did you have your greatest physical or emotional growth spurt? What was it like?
2. Who is the most courageous person you have ever known? How was that courage shown?

DIGGING IN

1. Explain the sharp contrast between what the lame man asked for and what Peter and John gave him.
2. How did Peter keep the attention of his listeners on Jesus, the source of his power, and away from himself as the miracle worker?
3. What did you learn about the different names of Jesus that Peter used and the power of His name?
4. Why did the Jewish leaders arrest Peter and John? What did they hope to accomplish by their arrest?

141

5. What did the Jewish council have to admit about the apostles and the healing of the lame man?
6. How did the early believers respond to the first persecution they experienced?
7. Why was there such an outpouring of generosity among the early believers?
8. Why do you think the sin of Ananias and Sapphira was so serious in the eyes of God?
9. How did the Ananias and Sapphira incident affect the reputation of the believers in Jesus?
10. Why do you think the Lord wanted the apostles to go back and preach in the temple after their deliverance from prison?
11. Why did the early believers consider it an honor to suffer for Jesus?

LOOKING FURTHER

1. How can you help people who want more from life understand that Jesus offers more than they have dared hope for?
2. How can remembering the power of Jesus' name help you be bold in witnessing for Him?
3. Why do you need to be lovingly firm in insisting that salvation from sins comes only through the name of Jesus?
4. What can the example of the early disciples teach us about responding to rejection and persecution?
5. What do you think the Ananias and Sapphira incident teaches about integrity in the church of Jesus?
6. How do you think we can determine whether we are obeying God when we resist human authorities?

MAKING PLANS

1. At what points in your personality do you know you need more courage?
2. What makes you chicken out when you want to witness for Christ?
3. What support do you need from a group of believers to motivate greater courage?
4. How do you need to adjust your reliance on the name of Jesus and the Holy Spirit to strengthen your courage?

LESSON 4
KICKED OUT OF THE HOUSE
Acts 6:1—8:3

SESSION AIMS

♦ To discover how a servant-leader stirred up ferocious opposition that cost his life
♦ To explore how opposition can cause a movement to expand
♦ To identify the cultural idols that are dangerous to reject or criticize.

Read through the questions in this *Bible Discovery Guide* and select those that you want your group to discuss. Supplement those questions with any of the ones provided below. Arrange the questions in the order that seems best for your group. Be sure to familiarize yourself with the feature articles in this portion of the *Word in Life Study Bible*. These helps can greatly enrich your group's insights into God's Word.

WARMING UP

1. When you were young, who was the outcast in your neighborhood or circle of friends? Why was that child rejected?
2. Since biblical times, what historical figure who gave his or her life for a cause seems most heroic to you? Why?

DIGGING IN

1. How did the early believers solve their first problem of tension between ethnic and cultural groups?
2. Why do you think Stephen faced more intense resistance than Peter and John had?
3. How did Stephen reason that Israel had historically rejected the spiritual leaders God gave them?
4. How did Stephen reason that Israel had historically ignored the messages God gave them?
5. How did Stephen reason that Israel had historically overvalued the temple?
6. What do you think the contrast between the rage of the Jewish council and the tranquility of Stephen meant?
7. Why do you think such intense persecution broke out after the martyrdom of Stephen?

LOOKING FURTHER

1. What qualities that make a good Christian servant also make a good Christian leader?
2. What factors do you think make some people more hostile to the message of Jesus than others?
3. What do you think are the sacred cows of modern culture that Christians risk persecution by criticizing?
4. When do you think you should avoid antagonizing a group of nonbelieving critics? Under what circumstances do you think you should firmly confront them?
5. If you faced harsh persecution, how would you look for the grace to respond as Jesus and Stephen did?
6. Why do you think opposition often causes a Christian or a church to grow?

MAKING PLANS

1. What are the major areas in which you would like to see your church standing up to contemporary culture?
2. What personal actions should you consider taking to help your church address needs in society?
3. How do you think standing up to contemporary culture would stimulate the health and growth of your church?

LESSON 5
THE GOSPEL MAKES STRANGE BEDFELLOWS
Acts 8:4—9:31

SESSION AIMS

◆ To note the ability of the gospel to attract all kinds of people
◆ To discover how believers struggled to include diverse people
◆ To evaluate our own openness to God's calling and commissioning of different kinds of believers.

Read through the questions in this *Bible Discovery Guide* and select those that you want your group to discuss. Supplement those questions with any of the ones provided below. Arrange the questions in the order that seems best for your group. Be sure to familiarize yourself with the feature articles in this portion of the *Word in Life Study Bible*. These helps can greatly enrich your group's insights into God's Word.

WARMING UP

1. What is the most unlikely pair of friends you have ever known? What made (makes) them such an "odd couple"?
2. Who is the most unlikely convert to Christianity you have ever known? Why did you think that person would never become a Christian?

DIGGING IN

1. Why was it so difficult to unite Jews and Samaritans as believers in Jesus?
2. What was wrong with Simon the sorcerer's perception of faith in Jesus?
3. How did the Lord guarantee that Jewish and Samaritan believers had to respect one another?
4. What evidence do you see that suggests Philip was readily available for the Lord's leading?
5. What evidence do you see that the Ethiopian eunuch was eager to believe in Christ?
6. Why do you think the Lord converted Saul directly rather than through a preacher or witness?
7. Why do you think the Lord sent an ordinary believer rather than an apostle to restore and baptize Saul?
8. How did the Lord move Saul away from Jerusalem so he could begin his unique ministry to Gentiles?
9. Why do you think the Hellenistic Jews of Jerusalem would not listen to the witness of Saul, their former star persecutor?

LOOKING FURTHER

1. How do power and prestige try to lure you away from humble Christian service?
2. What are the most serious racial and ethnic barriers your church faces?
3. What doubts do you tend to have about the faith of powerful people (like the treasurer of Ethiopia)?
4. What would your concerns be about the reported conversion of a vicious opponent of Christians?
5. How would you feel about attending a church made up of believers drawn from antagonistic racial groups, foreign countries, and fanatical fringe groups?

6. What kinds of instruction, fellowship, and service opportunities do you think would help unite such a diverse church?
7. God gifts and commissions leaders from every segment of the church. How would you respond to leaders from minority groups within the church? What unconscious biases would you need to resist?

MAKING PLANS

1. How could your church promote unity and fellowship among Christians from all ethnic and socioeconomic groups in your community?
2. What things do you think diverse groups of Christians should agree on in order to worship and work together? What kinds of differences should they accept and respect?

LESSON 6
"GOD DON'T MAKE NO JUNK"
Acts 9:32—11:18

SESSION AIMS

◆ To discover how God first incorporated Gentiles into the church
◆ To explore the role of leadership during monumental changes
◆ To assess how faithful witnessing will challenge our comfort zone

Read through the questions in this *Bible Discovery Guide* and select those that you want your group to discuss. Supplement those questions with any of the ones provided below. Arrange the questions in the order that seems best for your group. Be sure to familiarize yourself with the feature articles in this portion of the *Word in Life Study Bible*. These helps can greatly enrich your group's insights into God's Word.

WARMING UP

1. Tell about a time when you found out that a long-cherished belief wasn't true. How did you feel?
2. Who was an "ugly duckling" when you were a child that developed into a "swan" as an adult? When did you first realize this was happening?

DIGGING IN

1. Why do you think that the apostle Peter visited the small groups of believers in Judean towns like Lydda and Joppa?
2. As Peter got farther from Jerusalem, the miracles God did through him got greater until in Caesarea Gentiles were saved. How is this consistent with the overall theme of Acts?
3. Why did the Lord need to repeat the vision He showed Peter?
4. What gospel content did Peter share with Cornelius and his friends before they believed?
5. Why were the Jerusalem believers more concerned that Peter had eaten with Gentiles than that he had evangelized them?
6. Why do you think the early believers were so ready to believe the reports of the incredible works of God in Samaritan villages, on the Gaza road, in Judean coastal villages, and at Caesarea?
7. Why do you think God refused to allow the Jerusalem church to be comfortable with their deeply-held racial biases?

LOOKING FURTHER

1. Peter led the way in getting the Jerusalem church to accept Gentile believers as brothers and sisters. What role do you think leadership must play in reducing racial biases in churches?
2. What risks do you think leaders face who challenge the status quo in race relations among Christians in your community?
3. Peter also crossed lines of class, geography, diet, and politics when he went to Cornelius's house. To what kinds of people do you feel fairly comfortable witnessing? What kinds of ministry situations would make you very uncomfortable?

MAKING PLANS

1. How could your church initiate a worship and outreach partnership with a church of a distinct racial or socioeconomic group to express the rich diversity of the body of Christ?
2. How should your church respond to the leaders of the partner church?

LESSON 7
THE POT STARTS TO BOIL
Acts 11:19—13:12

SESSION AIMS

◆ To see how God moved the center of gospel activity from Jerusalem to Antioch
◆ To contrast the survival mode of the Jerusalem church with the expansion mode of the Antioch church
◆ To explore the "mode" we operate in privately and the "mode" our church operates in
◆ To evaluate our openness to being "sent" by God on a mission suited to our gifts and abilities.

Read through the questions in this *Bible Discovery Guide* and select those that you want your group to discuss. Supplement those questions with any of the ones provided below. Arrange the questions in the order that seems best for your group. Be sure to familiarize yourself with the feature articles in this portion of the *Word in Life Study Bible*. These helps can greatly enrich your group's insights into God's Word.

WARMING UP

1. In your community, what is the proud old neighborhood and what is the fast-growing part of town? How do they feel about one another?
2. Do you love computers and the latest electronic gadgetry or do you avoid them? Why?

DIGGING IN

1. How did Antioch become the hub of innovative witness for Jesus?
2. How did Barnabas continue to be an encourager of believers and a facilitator of growth and expansion?
3. While Antioch was welcoming the gospel, what was the spiritual climate like for the gospel in Jerusalem?
4. How were the energies of the Jerusalem church channeled while its leaders were persecuted by Herod?
5. Did Peter and the praying church expect God to deliver him? Why do you reach that conclusion?
6. Why do you think Peter left Jerusalem after Herod tried to kill him?
7. Why do you think God chose to judge Herod for his arrogance when so many other wicked rulers have survived?

8. Why do you think the Lord gave so many gifted leaders to the church of Antioch?
9. How did the ministry of Barnabas and Saul in Cyprus illustrate the spiritual relations they would have in the future with Jews and Gentiles?

LOOKING FURTHER

1. Both James and Peter were godly men; James died and Peter was rescued. How should you face the tragedies of life when you don't know for sure that God will keep you from suffering?
2. What kind of judgment do proud and arrogant people invite into their lives through their sinful attitudes and actions?
3. When you think about the future of the church, do you tend to think in terms of survival (like Jerusalem) or in terms of aggressive expansion (like Antioch)? Why?
4. How do the circumstances of your church shape your attitudes about its future, and how do your attitudes toward its future shape the circumstances of your church?

MAKING PLANS

1. What do you think are your spiritual gifts and abilities to use for the benefit of the body of Christ?
2. What do you think is the greatest asset of each member of your study group for ministry?
3. In terms of your own assessment and the opinion of the group, what kind of ministry could you carry out in a missions setting to advance the spread of the gospel?
4. If you could go to any part of the world for a month as a short-term missionary, where would you like to go? Where could you find out how to make that dream a reality?

LESSON 8
"THE WALLS CAME ATUMBLIN' DOWN"
Acts 13:13—15:35

SESSION AIMS

◆ To understand the threat Jewish communities felt from the aggressive Christian missionaries

♦ To explore different Gentile reactions to the gospel
♦ To analyze the decision of the Jerusalem council
♦ To identify "culture clashes" within our church and examine ways of resolving them

Read through the questions in this *Bible Discovery Guide* and select those that you want your group to discuss. Supplement those questions with any of the ones provided below. Arrange the questions in the order that seems best for your group. Be sure to familiarize yourself with the feature articles in this portion of the *Word in Life Study Bible*. These helps can greatly enrich your group's insights into God's Word.

WARMING UP

1. Has anyone seen a crowd of people lose control and begin to act like a mob? How did you feel at the time?
2. When you were a child, what story did you love to hear again and again? Why did you like it?

DIGGING IN

1. How did Paul use the history of Israel to show the Jews of Pisidian Antioch that Jesus was the promised Messiah?
2. How did Paul and Barnabas use Old Testament Scripture to back up their claims about Jesus?
3. Why do you think the Jews of Pisidian Antioch were so disturbed by the popularity of the apostles' message about Jesus?
4. Why do you think the Jewish leaders actively opposed the appeal of Paul and Barnabas to the Gentiles?
5. How did the Gentiles respond to the gospel in Pisidian Antioch? in Iconium? in Lystra?
6. How could the Lystrans stone Paul when a short time before they had wanted to worship him as a god?
7. What was the dispute that necessitated the council in Jerusalem?
8. What parts did Peter and James play in resolving the dispute over how Gentiles could become Christians?
9. How did the Jerusalem council decision address the "truth issue" and the "love issue" of Gentile conversion?

LOOKING FURTHER

1. Why do you think some unbelievers get uncomfortable today when Christian ministries are visibly successful?

2. How do you think community attitudes and traditions affect the response of the whole town to the gospel?

3. What do you think a church or evangelistic team should know about your town before attempting a major outreach ministry?

4. How do you think the Jerusalem council succeeded in resolving the issue facing the church and in maintaining the unity of the group?

5. What are some of the tensions between cultural and biblical teachings facing the church today? What are some "truth issues" and "love issues" involved in them?

MAKING PLANS

1. What "culture clash" do you think poses the greatest threat to the ministry of your church?

2. What do you think would be the best way to make a unified and biblical response to the issue?

3. What role do you think the leaders of your church should play to ensure harmony?

LESSON 9
"To Boldly Go Where No Man Has Gone Before"
Acts 15:36—17:34

SESSION AIMS

◆ To compare differing motives for faith in Christ
◆ To compare differing motives for rejecting Christian missionaries
◆ To explore ways of increasing the probability that our witness will be accepted by others

Read through the questions in this _Bible Discovery Guide_ and select those that you want your group to discuss. Supplement those questions with any of the ones provided below. Arrange the questions in the order that seems best for your group. Be sure to familiarize yourself with the feature articles in this portion of the _Word in Life Study Bible_. These helps can greatly enrich your group's insights into God's Word.

WARMING UP

1. Describe an experience from your past that made you feel like a pioneer.

2. What's the most unusual or unexpected place you have heard music? How did you respond to it?

DIGGING IN

1. How did God create two missionary teams to multiply His outreach?
2. How did the Lord steer Paul, Silas, and Timothy from Asia to Macedonia in Europe?
3. Describe the diverse backgrounds and conversion experiences of Lydia, the slave girl, and the jailer.
4. Compare and contrast the opposition and rejection Paul and Silas experienced in Philippi, Thessalonica, and Berea.
5. From what is said about the first converts, what would you expect each of these churches to be like: Philippi, Thessalonica, and Berea?
6. What were Athens and the Athenians like?
7. What was the main point Paul tried to make in his address to the Athenian council?
8. Why did most of the intellectual Athenians dismiss Paul without taking his message seriously?

LOOKING FURTHER

1. How many different motives for rejecting the missionaries do you see in Acts 16—17? What do you think are the primary reasons people around you react negatively to Christians who share their faith?
2. How many different motives for responding to the missionaries Paul and Silas do you see in Acts 16—17? What do you think are the primary reasons people around you respond positively to Christians who share their faith?
3. What are the unique challenges of witnessing to intellectuals? How do you think the gospel should be presented to them?
4. What can we do to increase the likelihood that people we share Christ with will hear and understand our witness whether or not they respond with faith in Him?

MAKING PLANS

1. Who is presently your biggest challenge as you look for opportunities to present the gospel to your friends and associates?
2. What factors in this relationship and situation could lead to rejection of your witness?
3. How can you be sensitive and tactful when the Lord gives you the chance to share Christ with this person?

LESSON 10
DEEP ROOTS IN NEW SOIL
Acts 18:1—20:38

SESSION AIMS

◆ To explore how Paul based his ministry from major urban centers
◆ To observe the maturity and complexity of these later ministries of Paul
◆ To assess our commitment to communicating the gospel to the cities of our area and the world

Read through the questions in this _Bible Discovery Guide_ and select those that you want your group to discuss. Supplement those questions with any of the ones provided below. Arrange the questions in the order that seems best for your group. Be sure to familiarize yourself with the feature articles in this portion of the _Word in Life Study Bible_. These helps can greatly enrich your group's insights into God's Word.

WARMING UP

1. What city of the world has made the strongest impression on you? How did it do this?
2. Of the communities you've lived in, which one did you like best? Why?

DIGGING IN

1. How did leadership, location, and divine protection combine to make Paul's ministry in Corinth his most productive up to that time?
2. Why was Gallio's ruling so helpful to the church and so frustrating to the Jewish authorities?
3. Describe the extent and depth of the ministry of Priscilla and Aquila in Corinth and Ephesus.
4. What did the incomplete theology of Apollos and the disciples of John the Baptist suggest about the need of teachers and apostolic writing in the early church?
5. How did Paul's intensive ministry in Ephesus impact the city and its province of Asia?
6. Why do you think Luke pointed out that the church was protected by Roman legal structures in both Corinth and Ephesus?

7. How did Paul work to strengthen the churches he had planted and their leaders?
8. What did Paul have to say to the Ephesian elders about his example to them and his warnings for them?

LOOKING FURTHER

1. What are the key cities within 250 miles of your home?
2. How would spiritual revival in those cities affect churches in other towns and rural areas?
3. What role do you think human planning and strategy play in God's work to reach a city for Christ?
4. What do you think are the major differences between a biblical view of reality and an occult view of reality?
5. What kind of legal protection do the laws of the land provide for Christian ministry?

MAKING PLANS

1. To what kind of Christian service are you as committed as Paul was to his long-term ministries in Corinth and in Ephesus?
2. What more could you do to strengthen and encourage those to whom you have ministered in the past?
3. What would you like to see your church do to increase its commitment to urban evangelism?

LESSON 11
YOU CAN'T GO HOME AGAIN
Acts 21:1—23:30

SESSION AIMS

◆ To imagine how God could use the danger Paul faced in Jerusalem to accomplish His goals
◆ To compare and contrast the hostility of Jerusalem with the protectiveness of pagan Rome
◆ To explore how God uses uncomfortable and even dangerous circumstances to direct our lives

Read through the questions in this *Bible Discovery Guide* and select those that you want your group to discuss. Supplement those questions with any of the ones provided below. Arrange the questions in the order that seems best for your group. Be sure to familiarize yourself with the feature articles in this portion of the *Word in Life Study Bible*. These helps can greatly enrich your group's insights into God's Word.

WARMING UP

1. Describe a time when you returned to a place that was important to your childhood and found it much different than you had remembered it.
2. Has anyone in the group ever outgrown a very close friendship that turned into an unpleasant relationship? How did you discover the friendship had changed?

DIGGING IN

1. Why do you think Paul and his friends interpreted the repeated predictions of trouble in Jerusalem differently? Who had the more mature view? Why do you think so?
2. What was the plan of the Jerusalem church leaders to defuse the widespread hostility toward Paul?
3. Why did that plan fail?
4. What roles did Judaism and Roman authority play in the riot centered about Paul?
5. In his defense to the mob, how did Paul try to show that he was living a life consistent with Judaism?
6. How did Paul lose the respect of his Jewish listeners; how did he gain the respect of the Roman commander?
7. Why couldn't the Jewish authorities agree on their charges against Paul?
8. How did God see to it that Paul got away from the dangers of Jerusalem to the relative safety of Caesarea?

LOOKING FURTHER

1. How did God use the dangers Paul faced to accomplish His purposes?
2. How can we approach difficulties with the same confidence that Paul expressed on his way to Jerusalem?
3. How has God used uncomfortable or dangerous situations in the past to direct your life or teach you important truths?
4. What sorts of spiritual training seem to come best through the trials and dangers of life?

MAKING PLANS

1. What trials are you going through presently? What difficulties may be on the horizon?
2. Who supports you during times of difficulty? Are there other people or groups you should rely on?
3. How can you strengthen your confidence in the protection of God and the purposefulness of your trials?

LESSON 12

GOD IN THE DOCK

Acts 23:31—26:32

SESSION AIMS

◆ To explore why the authorities did not release Paul
◆ To examine the testimonies of Paul to Roman authorities
◆ To discover why Paul appealed his case to Rome
◆ To explore how to utilize political and legal processes for the advancement of the gospel
◆ To evaluate our ability to serve God during long, dry spells of life

Read through the questions in this *Bible Discovery Guide* and select those that you want your group to discuss. Supplement those questions with any of the ones provided below. Arrange the questions in the order that seems best for your group. Be sure to familiarize yourself with the feature articles in this portion of the *Word in Life Study Bible*. These helps can greatly enrich your group's insights into God's Word.

WARMING UP

1. Has anyone here witnessed a dramatic courtroom incident? What was it like?
2. Was anyone in the group ever sent to the principal's office as a student? What was your principal like—stern, gentle, disinterested, etc.?

DIGGING IN

1. How did the Jewish authorities try to maneuver Felix into condemning Paul?
2. How did Paul defend his Jewishness and innocence before Felix?

3. How did Felix handle Paul's case?
4. How did the Jewish leaders try to maneuver Felix's successor Festus into condemning Paul?
5. How did Paul outmaneuver his Jewish accusers?
6. What kind of help did Festus want from King Agrippa?
7. How did Paul evangelize King Agrippa during the defense he made before him?
8. What was the outcome of Agrippa's hearing of Paul's case?

LOOKING FURTHER

1. Why do you think the Roman authorities neither condemned nor released Paul?
2. What do you imagine Paul did during the two years of his confinement in Caesarea?
3. How can God use the long, dry periods of our lives in positive ways? What do our attitudes need to be during those times?
4. When do you think that God expects His people to accept wrong, and when do you think He expects us to utilize legal means to protect and advance the cause of the gospel?

MAKING PLANS

1. What Christian legal-political action group(s) do you admire? How can you participate or assist in their activities?
2. Who do you know that is going through a long, dry period in his or her life? What practical help can you provide to make this ordeal more bearable?

LESSON 13
JOURNEY TO THE CENTER OF THE EARTH
Acts 27:1—28:31

SESSION AIMS

◆ To observe how God brought Paul into prominence during his transport as a prisoner
◆ To explore the divine protection Paul received because he had a mission to accomplish

◆ To describe the entrance of the gospel into the capital of the Roman Empire
◆ To identify the "Rome" of our lives—the person, group, or place toward which God is directing us
◆ To connect the story of our church to the story of Acts

Read through the questions in this *Bible Discovery Guide* and select those that you want your group to discuss. Supplement those questions with any of the ones provided below. Arrange the questions in the order that seems best for your group. Be sure to familiarize yourself with the feature articles in this portion of the *Word in Life Study Bible*. These helps can greatly enrich your group's insights into God's Word.

WARMING UP

1. What is the most unusual long trip you ever made? What happened on it?
2. Has anyone in the group ever been seasick? What do you remember most about the incident?

DIGGING IN

1. As the disastrous journey to Rome advanced, how did Paul assume more and more authority among the travelers?
2. Why was Paul's sea voyage from Caesarea to Rome so dangerous?
3. What were the crews of the ships doing to minimize the effects of the weather?
4. What steps did the crew take to save the ship once the gale was driving it?
5. Why do you think God saved everyone on the ship with Paul, Luke, and Aristarchus?
6. What do you think the stay on Malta meant to Paul? to the Roman escorts? to the Maltese?
7. What do you think it meant to Paul to be met by a delegation of Roman Christians and escorted by them into the capital city?
8. Why do you think the Roman Jews were subdued in their opposition to Paul and the gospel of Christ?
9. How did Paul occupy himself during his two years in Rome?

LOOKING FURTHER

1. How do you think the difficulties of the trip to Rome helped prepare Paul for the trials and (eventual) martyrdom that lay before him?

2. How do you react to emergencies? In those situations, how can you better put into practice the truth you know about God's love and protection?

3. Luke left Acts rather open-ended. Every generation adds another chapter. How is your church extending the gospel of Christ at home and to the end of the earth? What more would you like to see it do?

4. For a long time Paul had a strong sense that God was directing him toward Rome. What is the "Rome" of your Christian witness? What person, group, or place holds a special place in your heart that seems to be God-given?

MAKING PLANS

1. Who can you encourage by telling about what you learned from this study of Acts? Who else would benefit from these ideas?

2. What do you think is the most important action plan you've considered during this study? What have you done about it so far? What should be your next step?

3. What progress have you made toward the witnessing goal you wrote in the margin of your _Bible Discovery Guide_ at the end of Lesson One?

RESOURCES FOR STUDY LEADERS FROM THOMAS NELSON PUBLISHERS

McDonald, William. *Believer's Bible Commentary*. Excellent, easily grasped comments on all of the books of the Bible.

Nelson's Complete Book of Bible Maps and Charts. Excellent source of handouts and teaching visual aids.

Packer, J.I. *et al. Nelson's Illustrated Encyclopedia of Bible Facts.* A fully illustrated fact-finding sourcebook to the people, places, cultures, and events of the Bible. Fully indexed.

Nelson's New Illustrated Bible Dictionary. Descriptions (many illustrated) of people, places, things, and ideas of the Bible.

Nelson's Quick Reference™ Bible People and Places. A pocket-sized guide with thumbnail sketches of everyone and every place in the Bible.

Jenkins, Simon. *Nelson's 3-D Bible Mapbook.* A graphically exciting way to imaginatively experience the great events and places of the Bible through three dimensional, full color graphics with clear background commentary.

NKJV Exhaustive Concordance. An essential reference work for locating words and passages.

Wiersbe, Warren W. *With the Word*. A chapter-by-chapter Bible handbook with a warm devotional emphasis.

Wilkinson, Bruce and Kenneth Boa. *Talk Thru the Bible*. Overview information about every book of the Bible. Excellent charts and maps.

Vine's Complete Expository Dictionary of Old and New Testament Words. Ready nontechnical access to insight into the Greek or Hebrew words behind the English translation.

Vos, Howard F. *Nelson's Quick Reference™ Introduction to the Bible*. A pocket-sized Bible handbook that captures the highlights of every book.

Also Available:

THE WORD IN LIFE™ PRIORITIES FOR LIVING SERIES
Experiencing the Word in your Life:
      Making God's Word Relevant to Your World Today
Making Your Work Count for God:
      How to Find Meaning and Joy in Your Work
Living in a World of Wealth and Poverty:
      How to Manage Your Resources with Compassion and Integrity
Real Life, Real People:
      Drawing Comfort and Inspiration from the Experiences of Bible Personalities

THE WORD IN LIFE™ BIBLE DISCOVERY SERIES
A Guide to Exploring the Gospel of Matthew:
      Jesus, the Tender King and His Revolutionary Message
A Guide to Exploring the Gospel of John:
      Jesus, the Bridge Between the Eternal and the Everyday
A Guide to Exploring Acts:
      Ordinary People with an Extraordinary Witness
A Guide to Exploring Romans:
      Unleashing the Power of the Gospel